Essential
JOINERY

**The Fundamental Techniques
Every Woodworker Should Know**

Publisher: Matthew Teague
Copy Editor: Kerri Grzybicki
Designer: Lindsay Hess
Layout Designer: Jodie Delohery
Illustrator: Lindsay Hess
Photographer: Marc Spagnuolo
Indexer: Jay Kreider

Blue Hills Press
P.O. Box 239
Whites Creek, TN 37189

ISBN: 978-1-951217-05-1
e-book ISBN: 978-1-951217-16-7

Library of Congress Control Number: 2020934993

Printed in China

10 9 8 7 6 5 4 3

This book was previously published by Spring House Press. This is the first edition by Blue Hills Press.

Note: The following list contains names that may be used in *Essential Joinery* and may be registered with the United States Copyright Office: Association of Woodworking & Furnishing Suppliers; Festool (DOMINO); *Fine Woodworking; Fine Woodworking* Live; *Hybrid Woodworking;* International Woodworking Fair; Leigh (D4R); Marc Adams Woodworking School; *Popular Woodworking Magazine;* The Wood Whisperer; The Wood Whisperer Guild; William Ng School of Fine Woodworking; *WOOD Magazine; Woodcraft Magazine;* YouTube.

The information in this book is given in good faith; however, no warranty is given, nor are results guaranteed. Woodworking is inherently dangerous. Your safety is your responsibility. Neither Blue Hills Press nor the authors assume any responsibility for any injuries or accidents.

To learn more about Blue Hills Press books, or to find a retailer near you, email info@bluehillspress.com or visit us at www.bluehillspress.com.

Essential
JOINERY

The Fundamental Techniques
Every Woodworker Should Know

MARC SPAGNUOLO

BLUE
HILLS
PRESS

CONTENTS

INTRODUCTION

Mastering joinery really isn't about slogging through hundreds of obscure joints and mastering them all. It's more about building a strong knowledge of basic principles that can be applied to just about any joint design you can come up with. In this book I'll show you the five categories of joinery I consider essential for fine woodworking: butt joints; rabbets, dadoes, and grooves; mortises and tenons; half-laps and bridles; and dovetails. With this foundation under your belt you'll be able to apply that knowledge to build almost any piece of furniture. Even the most complicated joinery has its roots in the core techniques presented in this book. We'll look at the most common joints within those five essential categories and learn how to make them. We'll even repair a few mistakes along the way.

Before we dive into the cornucopia of delectable wood joinery, let's take a step back and talk about our motivations for building furniture. Is it because you're tired of crappy big box store furniture and think you can build something better? Is it because you took shop class in high school and the desire to build things has been with you ever since? Maybe it's because you have memories of a parent or grandparent who was a woodworker and the process taps into a special nostalgic corner of your brain. For many, the reason is even simpler: woodworking offers relief from the stresses of everyday life.

That certainly was the case for me when I got started back in 2004. I had an unfulfilling job I didn't enjoy and a very long commute. My

job as a technical service representative for an antibody company left me unchallenged, uninspired, and unmotivated. Woodworking provided a glorious microcosm of new experiences, skill sets, problems to solve, and tangible metrics by which I could measure my personal development. Oddly enough, the final product of my woodworking (furniture) wasn't a significant motivation for me. I actually didn't care much for wood furniture and my first five or six projects found homes with family and friends.

I grew up as a city boy in New Jersey with a mom and step dad who didn't think it was weird at all to fill our home with country music and country-style furniture: red oak as far as the eye could see, and the sounds of George Jones streaming through the security bars in the windows. By the time I left the nest, I promised myself I would only fill my home with furniture made of metal and glass. Apparently "cold and uninviting" was the mood I was shooting for. It wasn't until later in my woodworking career that I started to get comfortable with the idea of filling my home with my creations. And today, I find myself in an office trimmed with alder at a desk made of cherry with striking sapwood accents. I guess I should just come out and say it: I love wood. But even though I am now fortunate enough to be surrounded by furniture of my own making, I still get the lion's share of my enjoyment from the woodworking process itself: specifically, the crafting of fine joinery.

On the surface, joinery is just a means by which parts are held together. But a well-executed wood joint does much more than that. Allow me to employ an analogy: When a band plays, most people simply hear the song. But to a musician, a song is heard as the sum of its parts: guitar, bass, drums, and vocals. When the instruments are played well and the singer has a pleasant voice, the song will likely sound decent. But the real magic happens when the musicians work well together: when the bass and drums find the pocket and create an undeniably solid rhythm; when the guitar melody flirts with the vocal pattern so they become inseparable. These are the things that separate good music from great music. So it is with furniture. The joinery is what makes furniture more than just a collection of parts. It's where the furniture comes to life and reveals the personality, love, and pride that went into making it.

You might think I'm a little goofy for placing so much importance on joinery, considering most people will never see it. But I don't do woodworking for pats on the back and accolades: I do it because I love the process.

Each joint is a little project in and of itself with its own challenges, risks, and rewards. When I apply that final coat of finish to a newly constructed table, I feel an incredible sense of pride knowing I did my best and my sturdy joints are nestled in the cozy homes I made especially for them. Am I romanticizing joinery too much? Perhaps. I'm trying to sell books here! But let's be honest, the world could certainly benefit from a little more romance, reverence, and yes, goofiness.

In the end, how much effort you put into your joinery is completely up to you. There's nothing wrong with butt joints, biscuits, and pocket screws. As long as you're making things you're happy with, you have my full support and respect. I do encourage all woodworkers to explore new and improved ways of doing things, including better joinery.

If you're like me when I first started, you're probably a little intimidated by all of the terminology and options in the world of joinery. Classic joinery texts are informative and exhaustive, but also overwhelming and sometimes short on details. My goal with this book is to demystify joinery by distilling the topic down to the most useful joints in the craft. I truly believe that if you can master these five essential joinery categories, you'll have the skill set to make just about any piece of furniture. We'll cover the process in a step-by-step fashion while showing you various ways to get the job done. Depending on your personal desires or tool collection, you might prefer one method over another.

So with that long-winded introduction, it's time to leave the world of motivations, intangible benefits, and country music. Let's head to the shop and make some joinery.

Chapter 1

BUTT JOINTS

In its simplest form, joinery is nothing more than a method for attaching one piece of wood to another. There's no more fundamental example of that than the humble 90° butt joint. My very first woodworking projects featured butt joints; I still use them today when the project calls for it. As you progress in your woodworking journey, you will likely move on to some of the more involved joints covered later in this book, but this is where it all begins.

It's important to note that a simple glued 90° butt joint is inherently weak. The end grain of one of your boards will soak up most of the glue, rendering the joint ineffective. This is why much of this chapter focuses on reinforcement methods for each joint.

SCREW-REINFORCED 90° BUTT JOINT

One of the most accessible ways to reinforce a basic 90° butt joint is to add screws. The screws not only hold the pieces tightly together but also add reinforcement because the screw penetrates both workpieces.

TOOLS

Square
Tablesaw
Miter gauge or cross-cut sled
Clamp
Drill with countersink bit
Bandsaw or plug cutter
Mallet
Flush trim saw
Plane or sanding block

1. Cut parts to desired size. It is critical that the ends are nice and square.

2. Though there are many other options for squaring stock, a tablesaw outfitted with a miter gauge or cross-cut sled makes it quick work.

3. **Apply glue to the end grain** and the face or edge of the adjoining piece. While the glue won't add a tremendous amount of strength, I never let my joints go naked.

4. **Confirm the workpieces are** square and adjust the clamp if needed.

5. **Use an adjustable** countersink bit to pilot-drill the screw hole while also creating a nice deep recess for a wood plug.

6. **Drill at least two holes per** joint. Since these will be visible in the final product, take care to arrange the holes so they are visually pleasing.

7. **Drive a screw into each** hole and remove the clamp.

8. **To cap off the screws, you can** use a short length of dowel rod (typically ⅜").

9. **For end-grain plugs (like** those cut from a dowel), apply glue to the holes and the plugs and tap them into place.

10. **A better alternative is** to use a tapered plug cutter. Drill into a piece of solid stock and pop out the plug with a screwdriver.

11. **For a tapered plug (from the** plug cutter), be sure to align the grain of the plug with the grain of the workpiece. Then comes the most exciting portion of any joint assembly: wait for the glue to dry.

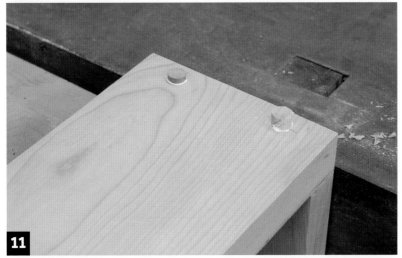

12. **Once the glue is dry, saw off** the excess using a flush trim saw and either plane or sand smooth. In the last photo, you can see the visual difference between an end-grain dowel (darker, on the left) and the face-grain piece from the plug cutter (almost invisible, on the right).

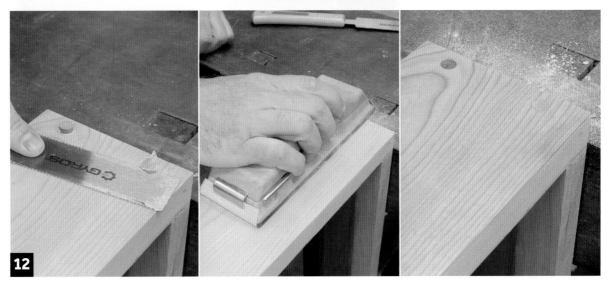

FRAME BUTT JOINT USING POCKET SCREWS

Pocket screws can make frame assembly quick and easy. Just cut your parts to length, drill the holes, and drive the screws. It's very common to see cabinet doors assembled with pocket screws.

TOOLS

Drill
Drill bit and driver
Pocket hole jig
Clamps

1. Arrange the parts to be jointed and label them clearly.

2. Lay out and drill pocket holes following the manufacturer's instructions on the non-show face. Place at least two screws per joint if possible.

3. Apply clamping pressure to the assembled joint so the boards don't shift. Glue is optional, but doesn't hurt.

TIP Avoid screwing into end grain. The pockets are usually drilled in such a way that the screw itself is biting into edge or face grain when the joint is pulled together. Screws are weak when driven into end grain.

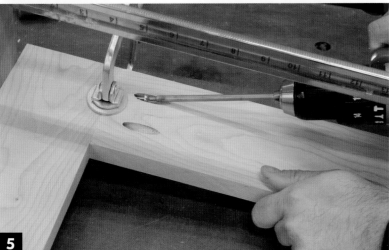

4. **Pocket screw companies** make handy clamps that help keep the joint nice and flush. These can be used in addition to the regular clamp.

5. **Drive the screws into place.** The screw helps close up the joint.

6. **This joint is easy to make** and surprisingly strong.

FRAME BUTT JOINT USING DOWELS

Another option for connecting frame parts is dowel joinery. Holes are drilled on both workpieces and premade dowels are inserted with glue. Dowels have the additional benefit of being completely hidden.

TOOLS

Dowel jig
Drill
Drill bit
Clamp

1. Arrange the parts to be joined and mark the dowel locations across the joint.

2. There are many dowel jigs on the market, but self-centering dowel jigs are the most useful.

3. Align the desired hole size with the lines on one of the workpieces and secure the jig.

4. Drill in the hole using the desired drill size with blue tape wrapped around the bit serving as a depth stop.

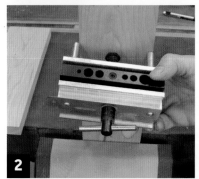

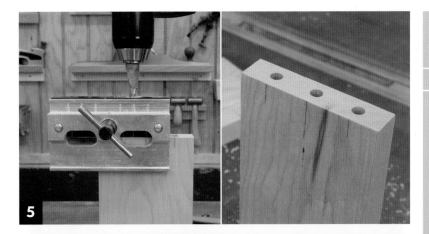

TIP You can make your own dowels using a simple device known as a dowel plate (a thick piece of steel with various common sized holes in it). Scrap wood can be cut or riven slightly oversized and then pounded through a dowel plate to create dowels of the desired diameter.

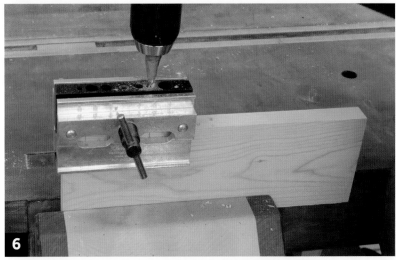

5. Move the jig to the remaining holes and repeat the drilling process.

6. Repeat the drilling process on the adjoining workpiece.

7. Insert dowels into each hole. For a more permanent connection, add glue and clamping pressure.

HOMEMADE DOWEL JIG ALTERNATIVE

A dowel jig is a nice convenience and offers increased accuracy and repeatability, but it is certainly possible to save a few bucks and make a shop-made doweling jig out of scrap wood.

1. **Lay out the desired hole** locations on a thick piece of scrap. Keep in mind, because this jig is made of wood, the holes will eventually wear out. Consider it disposable.

2. **Drill the holes as straight** and true as possible. Keep a large square nearby to give a visual reference.

3. **Glue another piece of** scrap to the reference side of the block to serve as a stop.

4. To use the jig, simply clamp it to the board, lining up the reference marks with the drill locations on the workpiece, and drill away.

5. After drilling the dowels in the adjoining piece, glue and assemble as per usual.

FRAME BUTT JOINT USING DOUBLE BISCUIT

Biscuits can make quick work of frame assembly, but for some applications, a single biscuit just doesn't seem strong enough. So let's add two biscuits in hopes of strengthening the joint.

TOOLS

Biscuit joiner
Straightedge

1. Arrange the parts to be joined and mark the center point of the biscuits.

2. On frame parts, there usually isn't enough width to put more than one biscuit side by side, but there is enough thickness to stack them. Set up the biscuit joiner fence so the slot will be off-center, with at least ⅛" of material between the slots.

3. Wrap the pencil line around to both faces of the adjoining workpieces.

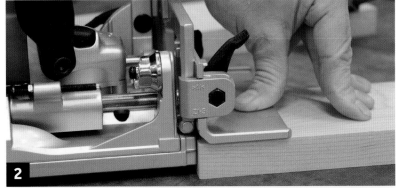

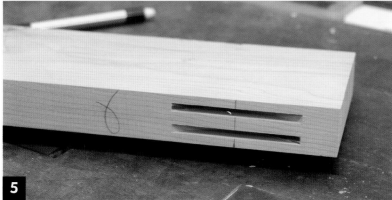

4. **Plunge into both workpieces,** once on each face.

5. **The slots should now be** symmetrical.

6. **Add two biscuits with glue** and apply pressure to the joint. The second biscuit doubles the glue surface area.

FRAME BUTT JOINT USING DOMINOES

A Domino joiner works in the same way as a biscuit joiner. The only difference is that the biscuits are replaced with loose tenons called Dominoes.

TOOLS

Square
Domino joiner

1. Arrange the parts to be joined and mark the center point of each Domino.

2. Set up the Domino fence so the mortises are centered on the thickness of the board and plunge at each pencil line on both adjoining pieces.

3. Insert Dominoes into the two mortises and assemble the joint.

TIP Domino tenons fit tightly into their mortises and can be very difficult to remove after a test assembly. Use a knife or some sandpaper to remove the little ridge on each side of the Domino and you'll have a much easier time inserting and removing the tenon from the mortises.

CASE BUTT JOINT USING POCKET SCREWS

Using pocket screws to reinforce case butt joints is standard fare and a great choice for kitchen cabinetmakers. It also works well in any case where face frames or other materials will conceal the screws.

TOOLS

Square
Pocket screw jig
Drill
Drill bit and driver
Clamps

1. **Arrange parts and label them** clearly. Lay out the screw locations on the board that will receive the pocket holes.

2. **Secure the board in the** pocket screw jig as per the manufacturer's instructions and drill the holes. Pay close attention to the face you're drilling into and how the screws will penetrate into the adjoining workpiece. Ideally, we want the screws driving toward the "meat" of the board, and not toward the edge. But sometimes, keeping the pockets hidden requires exceptions.

3. **Apply clamping pressure** to the joint so the boards can't move (glue is optional but certainly doesn't hurt) and drive in the screws.

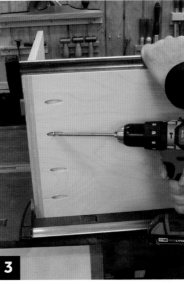

CORNER CASE BUTT JOINT USING BISCUITS

Another great joinery solution for casework is biscuits. Biscuits are premade football-shaped wooden discs that slide into perfectly sized slots cut by a tool called a biscuit joiner.

TOOLS

Adjustable square
Biscuit joiner
Clamps

1. With the two panels flat, butt them up end to end and mark the biscuit locations on both pieces at once. One piece receives slots on the face and the other receives slots on the end of the panel. In order to get a perfect flush joint without changing the settings on the joiner, transfer the marks around to the opposite face of the end slot panel.

2. Set up the biscuit joiner fence so that the biscuits are centered on the thickness of the panel.

3. Cut the slots on the end of the panel, with the fence on the back side of the panel.

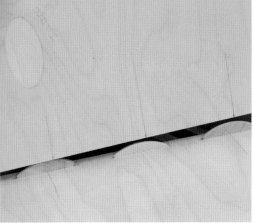

4. **The adjoining panel receives** slots on the face of the panel. Use a piece of scrap on the back side to help keep the biscuit joiner square and balanced.

5. **Insert biscuits into the slots.** I prefer #20 biscuits for most casework.

6. **Assemble the joint. When** being careful about which face of the board we use for reference, it's very easy to get a perfectly flush fit.

CORNER CASE BUTT JOINT USING DOMINOES

While the Domino cuts what is technically a loose mortise and tenon joint, for casework, the Dominoes function in the same way a biscuit does.

TOOLS

Domino joiner
Adjustable square

1. Arrange the parts to be joined and mark the center point of each Domino in the same fashion as when using the biscuit joiner (page 24). Plunge mortises at each pencil location on both workpieces.

2. Plunge mortises into the adjoining pieces using a piece of scrap behind the work for additional support.

3. Assemble the joint.

4. Check for square and make sure the outside surface is flush.

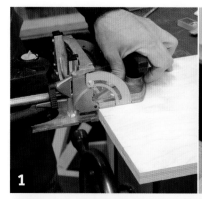

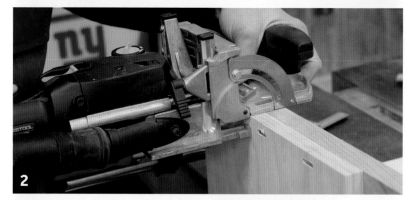
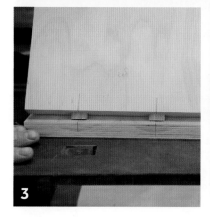

FLAT 45° MITERS: A FRAME

A flat miter joint is a butt joint where each piece is mitered at an angle (usually 45°). The most common and recognizable application for this is the classic picture frame. You'll also see flat miter joints in doors and other applications where a decorative frame is required.

45° MITERS *on* TABLESAW *Using* MITER GAUGE

TOOLS

Square
Tablesaw
Miter gauge

1. **Use a large accurate square** to calibrate the miter gauge, making sure it is perfectly perpendicular to the blade.

2. **Set the miter gauge to 45°.** Most quality miter gauges will be accurate at 45° as long as they are calibrated correctly at 90°, but we'll double-check using test pieces. Don't forget to slide the miter gauge as needed to keep it out of the path of the blade.

3. **Using a stop block on the** miter gauge, make a test cut on two jointed and planed pieces of scrap.

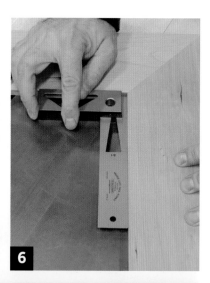

4. Place the 45° miters together to form a 90° corner and check for square. If the miter gauge is off, this measuring method makes it easy to see because your error is essentially doubled.

5. Set the gauge slightly to the side of the 45° notch and test cut again.

6. Now the two 45° cuts result in a perfect 90° corner.

7. Cut the actual workpieces using stop on the miter gauge.

8. Save those little triangle offcuts for clamping help later.

9. The miters should be nice and even when held side by side.

45° FLAT MITERS *with* MITER SAW

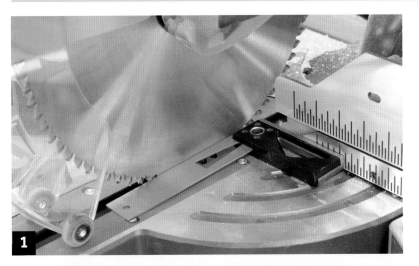

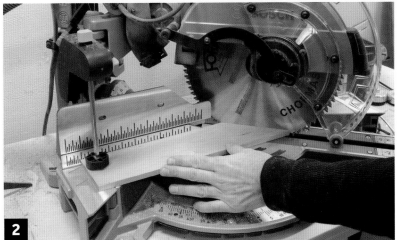

TOOLS

Miter saw
Square
Clamp

1. **Use a reliable square to make** sure the miter saw fence is square to the blade.

2. **Adjust the saw to 45° and** use two jointed and planed pieces of scrap to make two test cuts.

3. **Put the 45° miters together** and check for square. As you can see, there is quite a bit of error to adjust for.

TIP When making precise cuts at the miter saw, it's a good idea to use a clamp. The workpiece won't move and you won't need to use as much hand pressure to hold the piece in place.

4. After adjusting the saw and making more test cuts, the gap is removed and you're ready to cut the workpieces.

5. Cut the workpieces to size using a stop block, if possible, for repeatability.

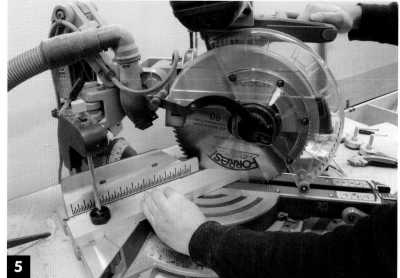

MITER ASSEMBLY STRATEGIES

Miter joints can be tricky to assemble with nothing more than glue and standard clamps. Because of the angles involved, the pieces tend to slide past one another and it doesn't take long before your carefully cut miters are overhanging and creating odd angles. Here are two of my favorite ways to assemble miter joints.

BAND CLAMPS

Band clamps typically feature four corner cauls, a metal or fabric band, and a clamping head that tightens the whole assembly by pulling on the band.

TOOLS

Band clamp

1. Position the parts on a flat work surface and arrange the cauls in their approximate positions around the frame (one at each corner). With glue applied to each joint, slowly tighten the band clamp, making any slight adjustments needed to keep each corner aligned.

TIP Always do a test assembly with no glue just to double-check the workpieces and to familiarize yourself with the process.

ANGLED BLOCKS

TOOLS
Clamp
Mallet

To assemble a miter using a regular clamp, we'll need to use angled cauls so that the clamps are oriented perpendicular to each joint.

1. Use thick CA glue to attach the triangle cut-offs to the ends of the mitered workpieces. A layer of blue tape between the frame and the blocks will help prevent tearout when removing the blocks.

2. Apply glue to the miters.

3. Apply clamping pressure to each joint.

4. After the glue dries, use a mallet to pop off the glue blocks.

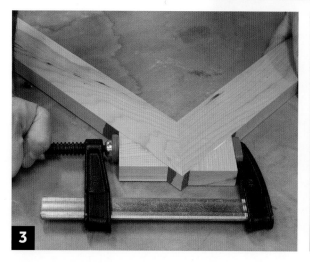

REINFORCING FLAT MITER JOINTS

Miter joints are essentially butt joints that are cut on an angle. As we know, butt joints are not very strong with glue alone so miter joints are often reinforced for the sake of durability. Fortunately, the reinforcement can also be a beautiful decorative element.

MITER KEY REINFORCEMENT *with* SIMPLE GUIDES

TOOLS

Adjustable square
Tablesaw
Square tooth blade
Clamps

Miter keys are thin strips of wood that are inserted into the miter joint after the joint is glued up.

1. **Mark a 45° V shape on the** face of a piece of plywood or MDF.

2. **Place the frame on the** plywood using the lines. At the bottom frame corner, use a small piece of double-stick tape or a dab of CA glue to secure the frame.

3. **Add two clamps and use a** tall fence on the tablesaw if you have one. Raise the blade so it goes at least halfway into the miter joint and make the cut.

4. **The slot is usually centered** along the thickness, though you have some creative flexibility. Use a square-tooth blade. The slot will provide a much nicer-looking joint than an alternating bevel blade.

MITER KEY REINFORCEMENT *with* TENONING JIG

1. Set the tenoning jig back support to 45° and clamp the workpiece in place.

2. Align the blade with the center of the workpiece (or off-center if you prefer) and raise the blade to at least halfway into the miter joint, then make the cut.

If you have a tenoning jig, miter keys are incredibly easy to make.

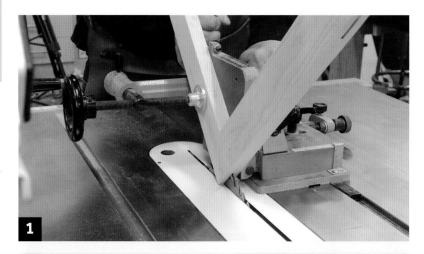

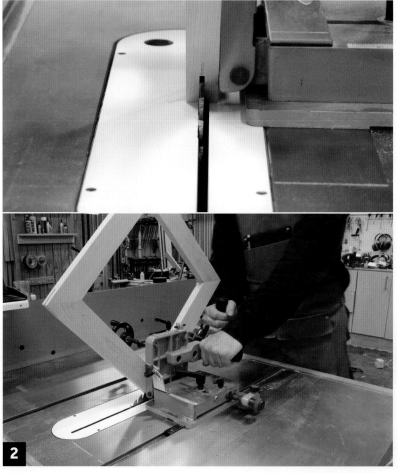

MITER KEY REINFORCEMENT *with* HOMEMADE CRADLE

If you make a lot of miter keys for frames and boxes, you might consider constructing a shop-made cradle. A cradle provides safe and repeatable results.

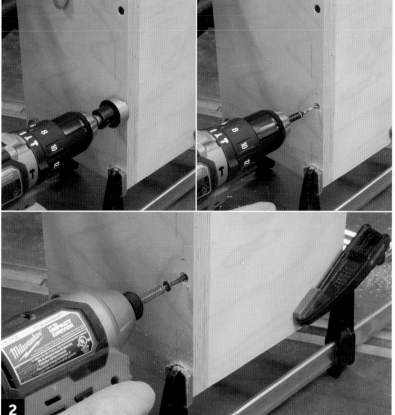

TOOLS

Adjustable square
Drill
Countersinking drill bit
and driver
Clamps

1. **You'll need four pieces of** sheet good stock to make the cradle. The type of sheet good isn't critical—MDF or plywood are both good choices. The dimensions are also not critical; shown are two center pieces at 7 x 11" and sides at 8 x 16". Glue the two center boards together at a right angle.

2. **Pilot-drill and countersink** screws to hold the center boards together.

TIP Countersink bits are often too short to drill the pilot hole fully into the adjoining piece. I like to use a separate drill bit to increase the depth of the pilot hole.

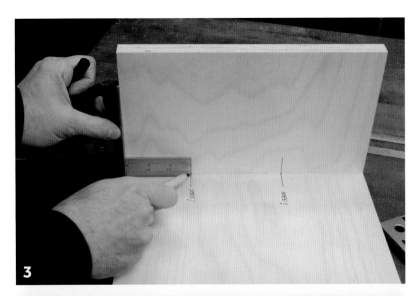

3. On the inside of the center pieces, clearly mark the locations of the screws to remind yourself *not* to cut through them later.

4. On the side pieces, draw two 45° lines from the center point.

5. Pilot-drill and countersink for screws about ⅜" inside of the pencil lines.

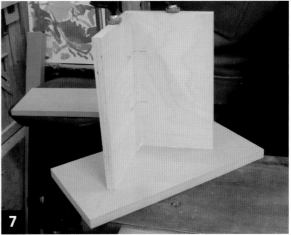

6. Make a glue line on the inside of one of the side pieces and drop the center piece in place.

7. Clamp the center piece in place.

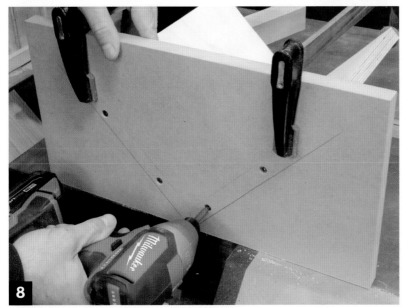

8. Drive screws into the drilled holes, making sure they're countersunk below the face of the stock.

9. Apply a bead of glue to the other side and attach it with screws.

10. Turn the jig upside down and mark the desired center point for the key. On a ¾" piece, this would be ⅜" in from the inside face of the jig.

11. Use the pencil line to locate the fence and jig relative to the blade.

12. Depending on your screw placement, you may want to remove the lowest screws on the fence side of the jig to avoid any contact with the blade.

13. Clamp the glued-up frame to the side of the jig with the corner fully seated in the cradle, raise the blade to the desired height, and make the cut.

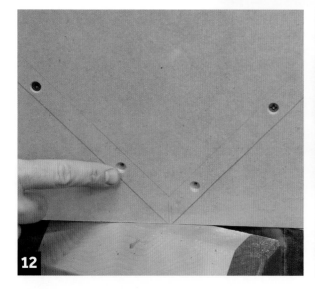

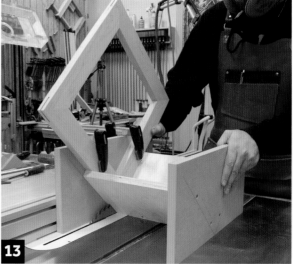

CUTTING + INSTALLING KEYS

Regardless of the method you use for cutting a key slot, the process for milling and installing the key itself is the same.

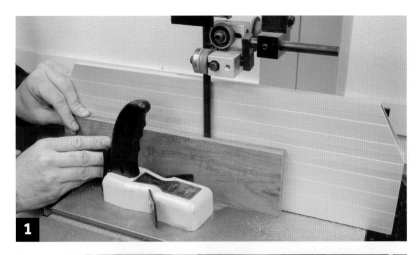

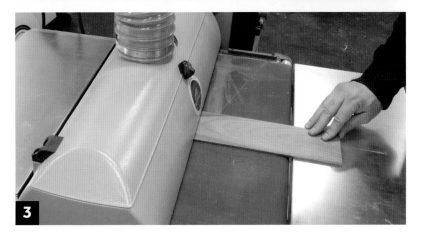

TOOLS

Bandsaw
Handplane or drum sander
Clamps
Flush trim saw
Sanding block or
handplane

1. **Resaw a piece of stock to just** proud of the desired thickness. The bandsaw can leave a rough cut, so you'll want an opportunity to smooth the surface while bringing it down to the perfect thickness.

2. **Smooth the thin strip at the** workbench with a handplane. Keep working until the piece fits into the key slot perfectly.

3. **A drum sander is a great** power tool alternative to smooth and thickness the key stock.

4. **The key should slide in easily** since it tends to swell once glue is added.

5. **The key stock can then be cut** into slightly oversized triangles. The grain should be oriented so it runs perpendicular to the miter joint in the frame.

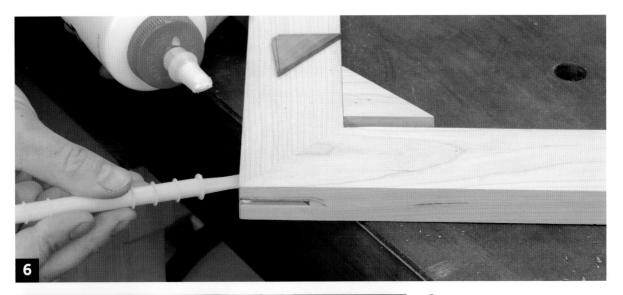

6. Apply glue to the inside of the key slot as well as to the key itself.

7. Press the key all the way into the slot so it bottoms out.

8. Using a triangle block as a caul on the inside of the corner joint, apply clamping pressure to keep the key in place. Note that you may want to dog-ear the corner of the key to help prevent crushing and splitting its fragile corner. Apply a second clamp to sandwich the joint together.

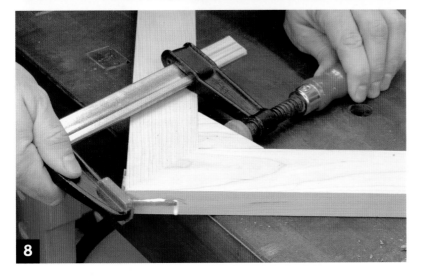

9. Once the glue is dry, use a flush trim saw to cut away the excess key stock.

10. Smooth the surface with a sanding block or a handplane.

11. A quick coat of finish highlights the decorative effect of the contrasting wood tones. For a less visible feature, use the same species of wood as the frame.

MITER REINFORCEMENT *Using* SPLINES

While keys are cut into the frame after the glue-up, splines are cut in the mitered pieces before the glue-up. The spline is a small strip of wood that helps keep the joints aligned and lends additional strength. There are three primary ways to cut them.

TOOLS

Tablesaw, tenoning jig, or router table with slot bit and miter gauge

Push pad

Adjustable square

Sandpaper

Clamps

Flush trim saw

1A. **Tablesaw using tall fence:** With a piece of sheet good for support, a mitered workpiece can be clamped at 45° and pushed over the blade to create a spline slot.

1B. **Tablesaw with tenoning jig:** With the back fence at 45°, the tenoning jig makes quick work of cutting a spline slot on a mitered workpiece.

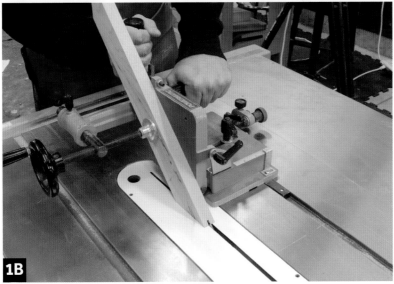

1C. **Router table with slot bit:**
A bearing-guided slot-cutting
bit makes spline slots quickly and
efficiently. Be sure to use a miter
gauge and fence to help support
the work.

2. **The spline stock is milled to**
thickness in the same way as in
the mitered key section on page
39. The spline strip is then cross-
cut into small individual splines.
The grain of the spline will run
perpendicular to the joint.

3. **The length of the spline isn't**
critical since it can be trimmed
after gluing, but the width has to
be perfect, otherwise there can
be gaps.

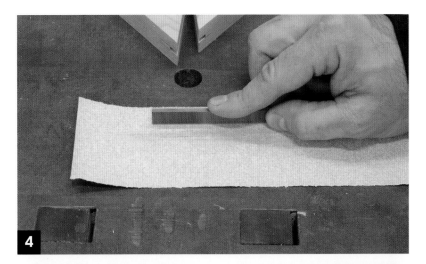

4. To make slight adjustments to the spline, use a piece of sandpaper on the workbench and rub the spline across the surface until the fit is perfect.

5. Assembly strategies shown on pages 31 and 32 apply here. The use of angled clamping blocks is shown.

6. The entire joint (miters and splines) are glued together all at once.

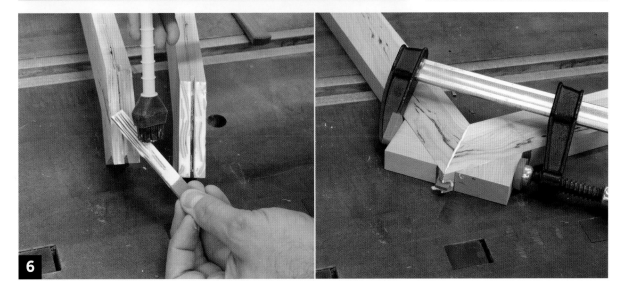

7. **After the glue is dry, use a** flush trim saw to trim away the excess spline stock.

8. **Sand or plane the surface** smooth on the outside corner.

9. **Use a sharp chisel to do** the final cleanup on the inside corner.

10. **In this case, a contrasting** species for the spline lends a decorative effect. If you want the spline to be less noticeable, choose a spline of the same species as the frame.

MITER REINFORCEMENT *Using* DOWELS

TOOLS

Dowel jig
Drill
Clamps
Drill bit

1. **Place the two mitered pieces** end to end and mark the desired dowel locations. Use at least two dowels per joint.

2. **Using a dowel jig (homemade** option on pages 18 and 19), drill each miter for dowels.

3. **Insert the dowels into the** miter joint and assemble using any of the techniques described on pages 31 and 32.

MITER REINFORCEMENT *Using* BISCUITS

TOOLS

Biscuit joiner

A biscuit joiner cuts slots in both faces of a miter joint, and a biscuit is used to join them together.

1. Put the two mitered pieces together to determine the ideal location for the biscuit(s).

2. With the workpiece clamped to the bench securely, plunge to create the biscuit slots.

3. Insert the biscuit into the slot and assemble the joint.

MITER REINFORCEMENT *Using* DOMINOES

For flat miter joints, a Domino joiner works in the same fashion as a biscuit joiner.

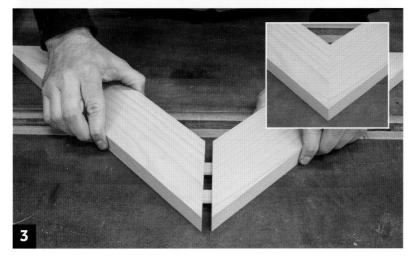

TOOLS

Domino joiner

1. Put the two mitered pieces together to determine the ideal location for the Dominoes.

2. Plunge the mortises on the appropriate pencil lines.

3. Insert the Dominoes and assemble the joint.

STANDING MITERS

A standing miter is a long miter joint, typically found in boxes and casework of all kinds. These joints work the same whether you're cutting a small jewelry box or a large chest. You may see the cut itself referred to as a *bevel cut*.

STANDING MITERS *with* TABLESAW

TOOLS

Tablesaw
Miter gauge
Square

1. Set up the tablesaw with the miter gauge perfectly 90° to the blade.

2. Tilt the blade to 45° and confirm the angle with an angle gauge.

3. Make bevel cuts on two pieces of scrap to confirm the setup.

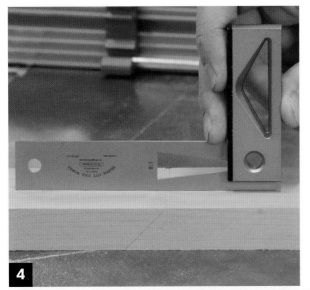

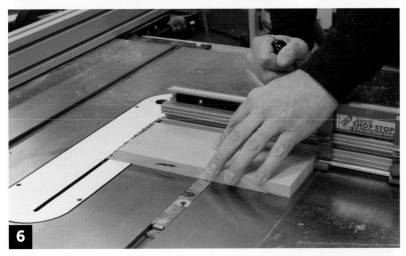

4. Put the pieces end to end to see how well they meet up. If there are any gaps, an adjustment should be made.

5. You can also test the setup by doing a dry assembly of the joint and confirming the two pieces make a perfect 90° corner.

6. Cut the miters on the actual workpieces with the help of a stop block for consistency.

7. This example shows a box. Bring all four pieces together to confirm 90° corners.

STANDING MITERS *with* MITER SAW

TOOLS

Miter saw
Miter gauge
Square

1. **Confirm the miter saw fence** is 90° to the blade.

2. **Bevel the head of the saw** to 45° and use an angle gauge to confirm the setup.

3. **Make two test cuts on** scrap stock.

4. **Bring the pieces together to** check for a 90° corner and adjust the saw if needed.

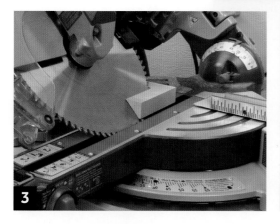

REINFORCING STANDING MITER JOINTS

Gluing up standing miters becomes easy with the simple addition of one non-traditional woodworking tool: strapping tape. This stringed tape holds well and allows you to pull joints closed using only hand pressure.

GLUING STANDING MITERS

1. Lay the parts end to end with the inside surface facing down. Using reinforced strapping tape, stretch a piece of tape over each joint.

2. Apply glue to the joints and slowly fold the pieces inward, bringing the miters together. The tape acts as a clamp and prevents the pieces from shifting.

3. Once the two ends come together, fold over the final flap of tape to secure the joint. If needed, a band clamp can be added to the assembly to provide additional clamping pressure. On smaller boxes, this usually isn't necessary.

STANDING MITER REINFORCEMENT *Using* KEYS

TOOLS

Tablesaw
Cradle jig
Bandsaw
Clamps
Flush trim saw
Sanding block or handplane

1. Using the tablesaw key sled, cut the key slots into the mitered box. Feel free to vary the placement and depth of cut to make an interesting pattern for decorative effect.

2. Size the key material to the slot.

3. Cut the key stock into oversized triangles where the grain will run across the joint.

After the box is glued up, keys can be added in much the same way as the keys mentioned on page 39.

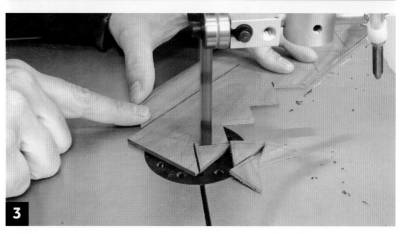

4. Put glue in the slot and on the key.

5. Use a clamp and a caul to press the key firmly into the slot.

6. Once the glue is dry, use a flush trim saw to cut off the excess.

7. Use a handplane or sanding block to smooth the surface.

8. A keyed joint can be quite attractive on a box.

STANDING MITER REINFORCEMENT *Using* SPLINES

TOOLS

Adjustable square
Tablesaw
Clamps

1. **Set the tablesaw blade to a** 45° bevel angle and cut a spline slot into the face of the miter. Then measure and cut the spline stock as described on page 44.

2. **Install the spline in the** joint with glue and clamp together with your preferred clamping method.

STANDING MITER REINFORCEMENT *Using* BISCUITS

TOOLS

Adjustable square
Biscuit joiner

1. **Place the miters end to end** and mark the locations for the biscuits.

2. **Adjust the biscuit joiner** fence to 45° and line it up with the pencil mark to plunge the biscuit slots.

3. **Insert the biscuit with glue** and clamp the joint together with your preferred method.

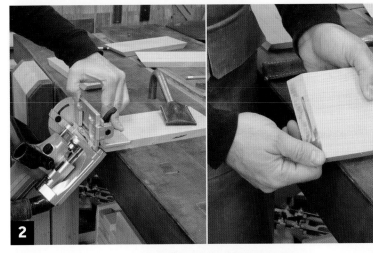

STANDING MITER REINFORCEMENT *Using* DOMINOES

TOOLS

Adjustable square
Domino joiner
Clamps

1. **Place the miters end to end** and mark the Domino locations.

2. **Set the Domino fence to** 45° and line up with the pencil lines and plunge the mortises.

3. **Insert the Dominoes** with glue and assemble the joint with your preferred clamping method.

SHOOTING BOARDS FOR HANDCUT PRECISION

As much as power tools are useful for their speed and power, hand tools can help finesse joinery to ridiculous levels of perfection, if you want. One handy classic device that facilitates this is called a *shooting board*. Shooting boards allow us to use a handplane to trim boards to the perfect desired angle.

1. **Adjust the fence on the** shooting board to the desired angle and double-check with a square.

2. **With the workpiece** against the fence and slightly overhanging the edge of the platform, run a handplane on its side in the channel on the bottom platform. A sharp plane will slice off the end grain like ham at the butcher counter.

3. **Check your results. Using** a combination square is a quick way to gauge your progress as you work.

Chapter 2

RABBETS, DADOES + GROOVES

These are essentially upgraded butt joints. By adding a recess to one piece so the adjoining piece can fit in, we gain a small amount of mechanical strength as well as additional glue surface. This makes the joints strong enough for cabinets and drawers. By the dictionary definition, all three are technically "grooves," but each one has particular characteristics that differentiate them in woodworking.

LONG-GRAIN RABBETS

Long-grain rabbets are partial-thickness cuts made on the edge or side of a workpiece going with the grain. The adjoining workpiece nests into the rabbet. This joint is commonly used in casework, doors featuring glass panels, boxes, and cabinet back panels.

TABLESAW *with* DADO STACK + SACRIFICIAL FENCE

TOOLS

Adjustable square
Tablesaw with dado blade
Sacrificial fence
Clamps
Push pad

1. On the end of the workpiece, use an adjustable square and a fine pencil to mark the width and depth of the desired rabbet. The width is typically the same dimension as the thickness of the adjoining workpiece. The depth varies, but aim for about half the thickness of the rabbeted workpiece.

2. Install a dado blade in the tablesaw at least as wide as the width of the desired rabbet. For example, if the desired width is ½", make sure the dado blade is ½" wide or greater.

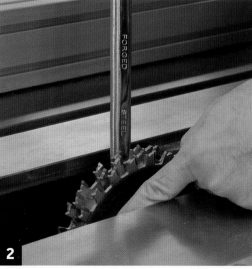

TIP Be sure to make obvious marks that indicate which face you'll be cutting into. It's all too easy to cut the dado on the wrong face.

A CLOSER LOOK

WHAT IS A DADO BLADE?

Some tablesaws can handle a special wide-cutting blade known as a dado blade (or stack). This wonderful tool consists of two outer blades with interior filler blades called chippers. With the various chippers and included shims, we can make cuts from ¼" to nearly 1" wide!

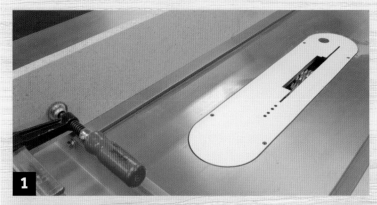

1. **Install a sacrificial fence** whenever cutting right up to the edge of a workpiece, otherwise the blade can cut into your primary fence. To make one you need only a piece of scrap at least ½" thick and a few clamps.

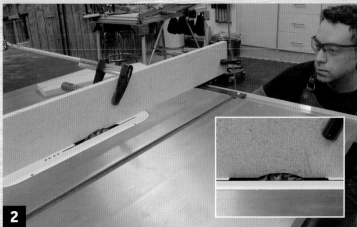

2. **Create the alcove for the** dado. Move the fence over the blade by about half the thickness of the sacrificial material. We don't want to get too close to our primary fence. Lock the fence in place, turn on the saw, and slowly raise the blade to about ¾" (higher for really large rabbets). We refer to this as "burying" the blade in the fence.

3. **Move the fence over** and set the blade height so it's just under the layout line.

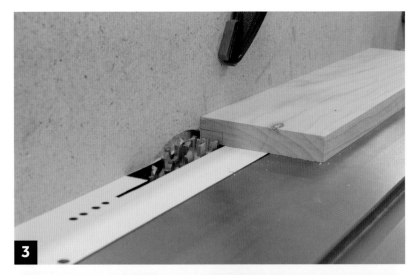

3. **With the workpiece against** the fence, adjust the fence position so the left side of the dado blade cuts just inside the layout line.

4. **Make the cut using a push** pad that allows you to apply consistent pressure downward and into the fence. A featherboard can help too.

5. **Test fit and adjust the fence** and blade if necessary. It's a good idea to be conservative on your first cut so that adjustments can be made at this stage without ruining the workpiece.

ROUTER TABLE *with* STRAIGHT BIT

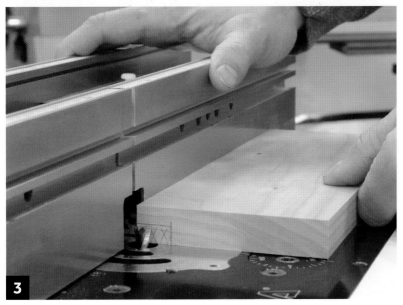

TOOLS

Adjustable square
Router table
Straight bit (spiral preferred)
Push pad

1. On the end of the workpiece, use an adjustable square and a fine pencil to mark the width and depth of the desired rabbet. The width is typically the same dimension as the thickness of the adjoining workpiece. The depth varies, but aim for about half the thickness of the rabbeted workpiece.

2. Install a straight bit in the router and adjust the height so it is just under the pencil line.

3. With the workpiece against the fence, adjust the fence position so the bit is just inside the layout line. If the bit is smaller than the width of the rabbet, you'll need to cut the rabbet in two steps.

TIP With a gloved hand or a piece of scrap wood, rotate the bit so that the blade tips are perpendicular to the fence for the most accurate positioning.

TIP If making dadoes ½" or wider, make them in two or more passes for the safest and cleanest results. That means having multiple fence positions, or having one fence position with two or more height adjustments.

4. Make the second pass. Adjust the fence so that the bit is just inside the layout line and make the cut to create the rabbet.

5. Test fit and adjust the fence and bit if necessary. It's a good idea to be conservative on your first cuts so that adjustments can be made at this stage without ruining the workpiece.

6. Test the fit with an adjoining workpiece and reposition the fence and cut again if necessary.

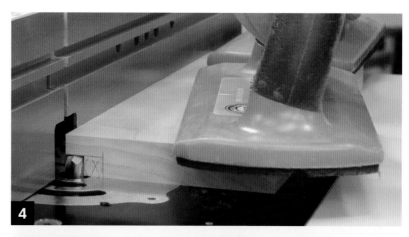

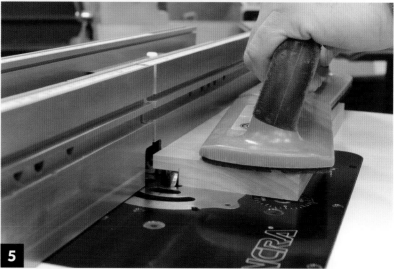

CROSS-GRAIN RABBETS

Cross-grain rabbets are partial-thickness cuts made on the end of a workpiece. The adjoining workpiece nests into the rabbet. This joint is commonly used in drawers, casework, and boxes.

TABLESAW *with* DADO STACK + SACRIFICIAL FENCE

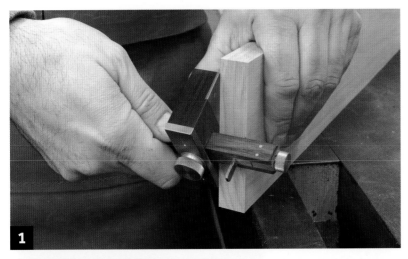

TOOLS

Cutting gauge
Adjustable square
Tablesaw with dado blade
Sacrificial fence
Clamps
Miter gauge

1. The rabbet's shoulder is defined by the thickness of the adjoining piece. Set a cutting gauge to that dimension.

2. Scribe the shoulder line on the workpiece that receives the rabbet, including the shoulder areas on the edges.

TIP Scribing with a cutting gauge isn't absolutely necessary, but it is recommended. Scribing not only provides a more precise line than a pencil, it also severs the wood fibers to help ensure a tearout-free cross-cut.

3. Mark the depth of the rabbet on the end grain of the workpiece using an adjustable square and a pencil. A cutting gauge works too, but this measurement usually isn't critical. Also, tearout isn't an issue on end grain and a pencil line is just easier to see. Aim for about half the thickness of the workpiece.

4. Install a dado blade in the tablesaw at least as wide as the width of the desired rabbet. For example, if the desired width is ½", make sure the dado blade is ½" wide or greater.

5. Install the sacrificial fence. A sacrificial fence is needed whenever cutting right up to the edge of a workpiece, otherwise the blade would cut into the primary fence. All you need to make one is a piece of scrap stock (½" thick or greater) and a few clamps.

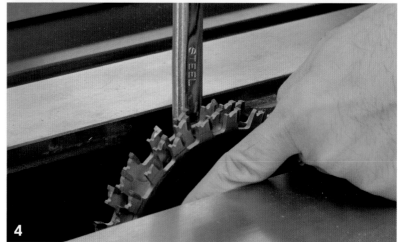

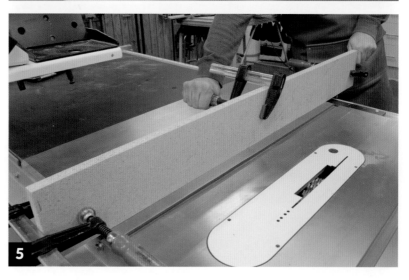

6. Create the alcove for the dado. Put the fence over the blade by about half the thickness of the sacrificial material. Don't get too close to the primary fence. Lock the fence in place, turn on the saw, and slowly raise the blade to about ¾" (higher for really large rabbets). This is referred to as "burying" the blade in the fence.

7. Move the fence out of the way and set the blade height so it's just under the layout line.

8. With the workpiece against the fence, adjust the fence position so the left side of the dado blade just barely touches the scribe line.

9. **With the help of a miter** gauge positioned 90° to the fence, make the rabbet cut.

10. **Test fit and adjust the fence** and blade if necessary. Be conservative on your first cuts so you can make adjustments without ruining the workpiece.

ROUTER TABLE *with* STRAIGHT BIT

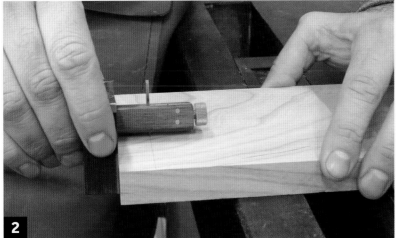

TOOLS

Cutting gauge
Adjustable square
Router table
Straight bit (spiral preferred)

1. **The rabbet's shoulder is** defined by the thickness of the adjoining piece. Set a cutting gauge to that dimension.

2. Scribe the shoulder line on the workpiece that receives the rabbet, including the shoulder areas on the edges.

3. Mark the depth of the rabbet on the end grain of the workpiece using an adjustable square and a pencil. A cutting gauge works too but this measurement usually isn't critical. Also, tearout isn't an issue on end grain and a pencil line is just easier to see. Aim for about half the thickness of the workpiece.

TIP If you don't use a cutting gauge to lay out your rabbet shoulders, I recommend adding a sacrificial auxiliary fence to your miter gauge. The fence will support the wood fibers and provide "zero clearance" during the cut. See Clean Cuts with an Auxiliary Fence (page 115).

4. Install a straight bit in the router table and adjust the height so the bit is just under the layout line.

5. Regardless of the bit size, set the fence so the bit just touches the shoulder cut line.

6. Cut the rabbet in stages, beginning with the end of the workpiece and ending when the workpiece is in contact with the fence.

RABBETS WITH A RABBETING BIT

Rabbeting bits are handy for making rabbets using nothing more than the bit and a router. Although they can be used to cut long-grain and cross-grain rabbets, the example shown here is a long-grain rabbet for a glass panel.

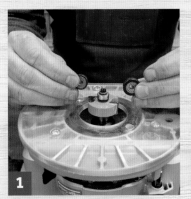

1. Install the appropriate size bearing on the rabbeting bit (different bearings produce different cut widths) and install the bit in the router.

2. With the router upside down and secured in place, set the bit height so it matches the thickness of the glass panel. Shown is a piece of scrap stock as a stand-in for glass.

3. Cut the rabbet with the bearing riding along the edge of the workpiece.

4. Test the fit and make any adjustments necessary to get the fit you're after. In this case, the panel should be flush to the frame.

DADOES

Dadoes are partial-thickness cuts made in the middle of a board across the grain. They are most commonly used in casework and are a great way to attach shelves inside a bookcase. You may also see them used in boxes and drawers.

TABLESAW *with* DADO STACK + MITER GAUGE *in* SOLID WOOD

TOOLS

Adjustable square
Tablesaw with dado blade
Handplane
Optional: Miter gauge and push block

1. Lay out the location of the dado along the edge of the workpiece, marking out the depth and width.

2. Set up the dado blade at the desired width. Because we're working with solid wood and have some control over the thickness of the adjoining board, the dado can usually be set up for common fractional sizes like ¼", ½", or ¾".

3. **Set the height of the dado** blade so that it is just under the layout line.

4. **With the workpiece against** the fence, adjust the position of the fence so the dado blade is centered between the layout lines.

5. **Cut the dado with the aid of** a miter gauge and a push block for additional downward pressure. Depending on the dimensions of the panel (specifically when there's enough reference surface against the tablesaw fence), you might be able to cut the dado safely without the miter gauge.

TIP In woodworking, it's important to know where you need to be exact and where you can settle for "close enough." When it comes to dadoes, the exact position of the dado is often less important than the fact that all related parts need to have the dado in the same exact spot. Use a bookcase as an example. It probably doesn't matter if the first shelf is at 12" or 12⅛", right? On the other hand, we better make sure that whatever height we cut the dado for the shelf, it's exactly the same on the other side. So be sure to batch out your joinery by cutting similar parts at the same time using the same setup.

6. **Test the fit by inserting the** adjoining panel in the dado.

7. **If the fit is too snug, plane,** sand, or scrape the panel down to final size. If the panel is already milled to size, you can sometimes get away with thinning the panel out just at the ends where it engages with the dado. Don't worry: it'll be our little secret.

8. **Insert the panel into the** dado to confirm the fit. Once you're happy with the results, proceed to cutting all similarly sized dadoes in your project.

TABLESAW *with* DADO STACK + MITER GAUGE *in* PLYWOOD

Cutting dadoes in plywood is similar to cutting dadoes in solid wood, but there are some key difference thanks to the inconsistency in plywood thickness.

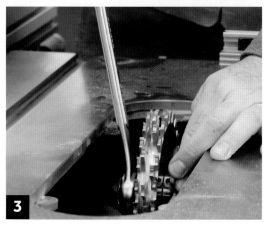

TIP Be sure to make obvious marks that indicate which face you'll be cutting into. It's all too easy to cut the dado on the wrong face.

TOOLS

Adjustable square
Tablesaw with dado blade
Optional: Miter gauge and push block

---

1. Lay out the location of the dado on the edge of the workpiece, marking out the depth and width with an adjustable square and a fine pencil.

2. Set up the dado blade to match the thickness of the plywood. Plywood can be very inconsistent from sheet to sheet, and even within a single sheet itself. Use an appropriate combination of shims and chippers to get the right dado width. Set the dado blade on a flat surface alongside a sample workpiece. By adding various shims and using fingers to test the height, you can usually get the dado blade very close to the perfect fit on the first try.

3. Install the dado blade into the saw and secure with the arbor nut.

4. **Make a test cut. Using a** pieceof scrap, cut a test dado. The depth doesn't matter at this point because you're only dialing in the width.

5. **Test the fit and adjust the** width of the dado blade as needed.

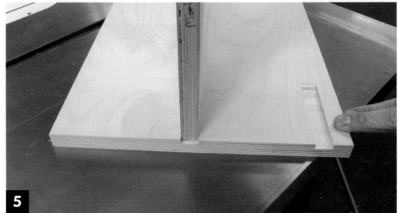

6. **Adjust the fence. With the** dado set to the desired height and the workpiece against the fence, adjust the fence so the dado blade is centered between the layout lines on the workpiece.

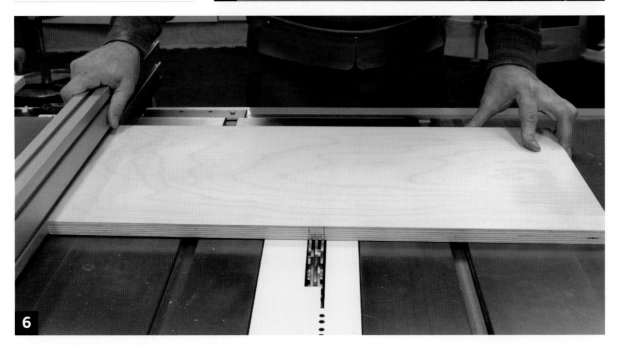

7. **Make the cut using a miter** gauge, if needed for stability. The miter gauge is critical on panels where the shorter dimension is against the fence as it helps prevent the panel twisting and kicking back. Clamping the panel to the miter gauge can add an additional layer of safety. Be sure to keep consistent downward pressure on the panel to combat any bowing or cupping.

8. **Insert panel into the dado to** confirm the fit. Once you're happy with the results, proceed to cutting all similarly sized dadoes in your project.

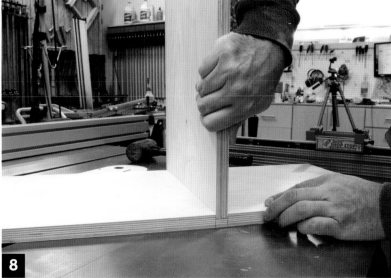

TIP Fitting a plywood dado requires a little forethought. Because plywood thickness is inconsistent and some plywood pieces become bowed, a "perfect-fitting" test dado may translate to cabinet parts that won't go together. For small parts (12" or less), aim for a snug-fitting dado; that is, one that requires a few taps with a dead-blow hammer to fully seat. For larger pieces, give the dado a few thousandths of an inch or more slack. If the workpieces are even slightly bowed, you'll be thankful for the extra room.

ROUTER *with* CLAMPING TOOL GUIDE *in* SOLID WOOD

TOOLS

Adjustable square
Router
Straight router bit
Clamping tool guide

1. **Lay out the location of the** dado on the face of the workpiece with an adjustable square and a fine pencil. The width of the dado will be dictated by the thickness of the adjoining workpiece.

2. **With the appropriate straight** bit mounted in the router, flip the router upside down and set the height for the desired depth of cut.

3. **Make a spacer block. To** make this and future setups easier, cut a spacer block where the width is exactly the distance between the bit and the edge of the router base. This spacer will come in handy any time you need to use this particular router/ bit combination and a clamping tool guide.

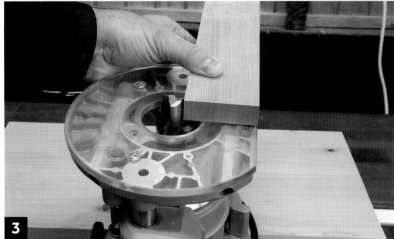

4. **Use the spacer block to** position the clamping tool guide the appropriate distance from the dado layout line and clamp the guide in place.

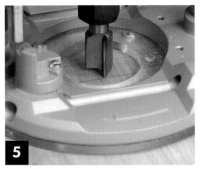

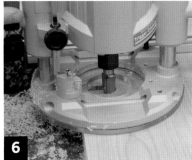

5. If the spacer block is cut to the correct width, the router bit will be indexed perfectly.

6. Cut the dado while applying firm and consistent pressure against the clamping tool guide.

7. The adjoining panel can now be finessed to fit in the dado.

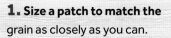

PATCH A MISPLACED DADO

A misplaced dado can seriously ruin your day. Cut a patch that fits snug into the dado and has the grain running in the same direction as the workpiece. This is most easily done by finding a board of the same or larger width and cross-cutting a piece off the end. In most cases, the repair won't be perfect due to inconsistent grain pattern and the two obvious lines that interrupt the grain flow. If the mistake is made on the inside of a case, however, this kind of repair is perfectly acceptable and saves a workpiece from heading to the dreaded scrap bin.

1. Size a patch to match the grain as closely as you can.

2. Glue the patch in place. Once the glue dries, sand or plane the patch flush to the workpiece.

ROUTER *with* CLAMPING TOOL GUIDE *in* PLYWOOD

TOOLS

Adjustable square
Router
Undersized plywood router bit
Clamping tool guide
Sanding block

Cutting dadoes in plywood is fundamentally similar to cutting them in solid wood, but the big difference is the fact that we have no control over the actual thickness of the material. Plywood is notoriously and frustratingly undersized by varying amounts, depending on the material and source. So, that sheet of ¾" plywood you just purchased is actually less than ¾". To combat this, router bit companies began making undersized plywood bits. If your plywood happens to be undersized by the same amount as the router bit, you're golden. If not, you're left with a tight or loose fit. But in many cases, the undersized plywood bits will get you close enough, and that's the type we'll use for this demonstration.

1. **Lay out the location of the** dado on the face of the workpiece with an adjustable square and a fine pencil. The width of the dado will be dictated by the thickness of the adjoining workpiece.

2. **Install an undersized plywood** router bit in the router. Because sheet goods are almost never exactly ¼", ½", or ¾", undersized plywood bits were created. In theory, these are awesome. In reality, the variable thickness of plywood means you won't always get a perfect fit. These will get you much closer than standard bits.

3. **To make this and future** setups easier, cut a spacer block where the width is exactly the distance between the bit and the edge of the router base. This spacer will come in handy any time you need to use this particular router/bit combination and a clamping tool guide.

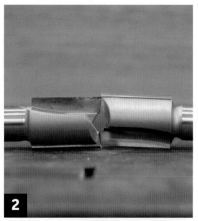

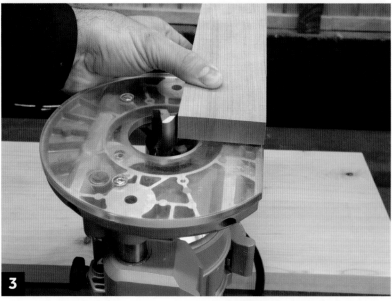

4. Use the spacer block to position the clamping tool guide the appropriate distance from the dado layout line and clamp the guide in place.

5. If the spacer block is cut to the correct width, the router bit will be indexed perfectly.

6. Cut the dado while applying firm and consistent pressure against the clamping tool guide.

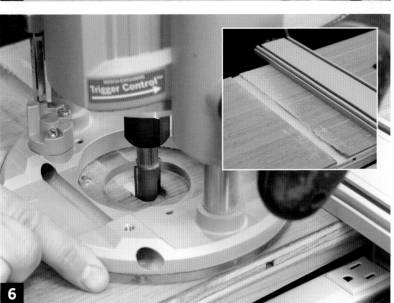

TIP If you don't want to buy undersized plywood bits, you can always make the dado in two passes. For instance, make two carefully aligned passes using a ½" diameter bit for a ¾" plywood dado.

7. Tame the fuzz. A cross-grain cut in veneered plywood usually translates to a buildup of fuzzy tearout along the dado edges. This is easily sanded away with a sanding block.

8. Test the fit with the adjoining workpiece. Unlike solid wood, you don't have an opportunity to size the panel to fit the dado. If you used a plywood bit, you're stuck with what you have. If doing multiple passes with a smaller bit, you might revisit the setup to fine-tune the fit.

ROUTER TABLE *with* STRAIGHT BIT *in* SOLID WOOD

While this section focuses on solid wood, the same operation can be used to cut dadoes in plywood by using an undersized plywood bit or making multiple passes with smaller diameter bits.

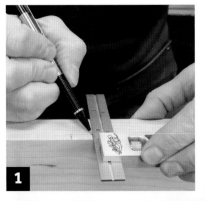

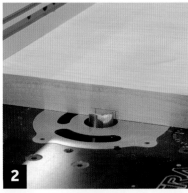

TOOLS

Adjustable square
Router table
Straight router bit
Miter gauge

1. **Lay out the location of the** dado on the edge of the workpiece, marking out the depth and width with an adjustable square and a fine pencil.

2. **Install the appropriate** diameter straight bit in the router table and set the bit height and fence positions according to the layout lines.

3. **Make the cut using a miter** gauge, if needed, for stability. The miter gauge is critical on panels where the shorter dimension is against the fence as it helps prevent the panel twisting and kicking back. Clamping the panel to the miter gauge can add an additional layer of safety. Be sure to keep consistent downward pressure on the panel to combat any bowing or cupping.

4. **The adjoining panel can now** be finessed to fit into the dado.

GROOVES

All of the previous dado operations can also work for grooves. The only difference is the dado runs with the grain, and is referred to as a groove. We won't be redundant by repeating that information here. Instead, we'll cover one of the most common types of grooves woodworkers cut: a panel groove. The panel groove is employed when making frame and panel cabinets as well as frame and panel doors.

TABLESAW *with* SINGLE BLADE

TOOLS

Adjustable square
Tablesaw

This is a "quick and dirty" method for perfectly centered narrow grooves (⅛ to ¼"). You don't use precise layout and you don't need a special sized blade. A cool tablesaw trick will generate a centered groove that's wider than the kerf of the saw blade.

1. Layout requires nothing more than a depth line and a center line on the end of the workpiece. With the workpiece against the fence, line up the blade roughly on the center line with the height just under the layout line.

2. Make the cut. The first cut with one face against the fence and the second cut with the other face against the fence. The resulting groove should be wider than the tablesaw blade kerf, but not quite wide enough for the panel.

TIP It's always a good idea to mill extra stock when milling project parts. Those extra pieces will allow you to do setups without risking your good project material.

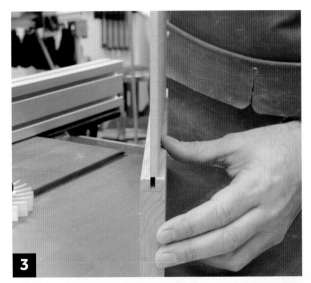

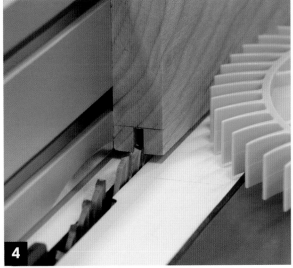

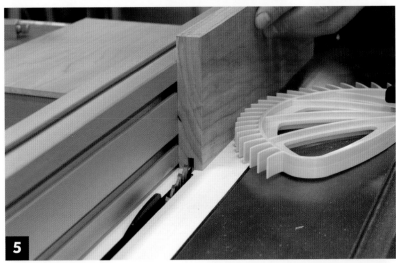

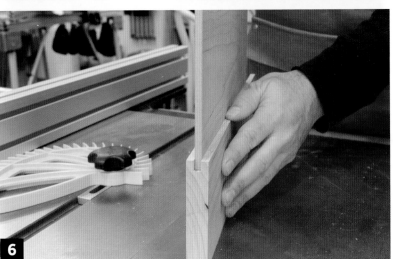

3. A test fit gives an idea of how much wider the groove needs to be.

4. Adjust the fence slightly. Just remember you will always make two cuts, so if your adjustment is 1/32", the end result will be a groove that is actually 1/16" wider.

5. Make the cut again.

6. Test the fit once again and repeat the process as needed. Keep in mind that if you have multiple workpieces to cut, you can now cut all of them with two quick passes, assuming the groove is 1/4" or less.

ROUTER TABLE *with* STRAIGHT BIT

TOOLS

Adjustable square
Router table
Straight bit

1. Lay out the location of the groove on the end of the workpiece and adjust the height of the bit to the layout line.

2. With the workpiece against the fence, adjust the fence position so that the blade is centered between the layout lines.

3. Route the groove. If making a groove that is wider than the diameter of the bit, flip the piece around 180° and make a second pass with the other face against the fence.

4. Test the fit of the panel. If the panel is solid wood and too tight, you may be able to sand or plane it to fit if it's too snug. If using plywood and the fit is too snug, you may need to adjust the fence to widen the groove slightly. In either case, if the groove is too wide and the fit of the panel is sloppy, it's probably best to repeat the setup process and try again. Good thing you used a test piece!

At the router table, you have the option of using various bit sizes. You can either use a bit that perfectly matches the size of the panel, or employ the two-pass method.

TIP With a gloved hand or a piece of scrap wood, rotate the bit so that the blade tips are perpendicular to the fence for the most accurate positioning.

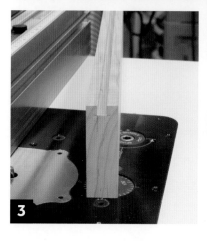

REINFORCING THE JOINTS

If you take a close look at a rabbet joint, you see the end grain of one board meeting the face grain of the adjoining board. While this is stronger than a simple butt joint, it might not be strong enough, depending on the application.

DOWEL-REINFORCED RABBET

Inserting dowels after assembly is a great way to beef up the structure while also allowing an opportunity for visual enhancement, especially if using a dowel of a contrasting species.

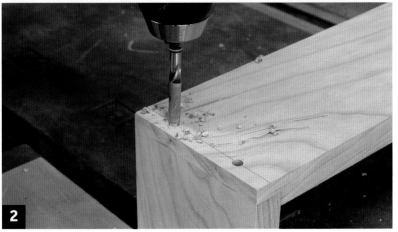

TOOLS

Adjustable square
Drill
Drill bit
Hammer or mallet
Flush trim saw
Sandpaper

1. Assemble the joint with glue. Once dry, draw a line representing the center of the adjoining board as well as crosshairs for each dowel location.

2. Drill the holes. Wrap blue tape around the bit as a depth gauge. Each hole is drilled deep enough to go through the rabbet and into the adjoining workpiece.

3. Cut the dowel stock slightly longer than the depth of the hole and apply glue to the hole and the dowel.

4. Drive the dowels until they bottom out. When using a metal hammer, you'll hear a change in the tone of hammer blow.

5. Use a flush trim saw to cut off the excess material.

6. Sand the surface smooth.

REINFORCED DADO

Dadoes can be incredibly strong, especially if talking about a cabinet or a bookcase where multiple dadoes and shelves are working together. But sometimes it's good to add additional reinforcement that prevents the panels from ever coming out of the dadoes. Reinforcement can be done with brad nails, screws, dowels, or a combination. Here is a favorite solution: screws capped off with wood plugs.

TOOLS
Drill
Drill bit
Countersink bit
Driver bit
Mallet
Flush trim saw
Sandpaper

1. **Drill through the inside of** the dado to mark the locations for the screws.

2. **Flip the panel over and drill** a countersink at each hole. Most countersink bits can be adjusted to make the hole slightly deeper, which is exactly what you want since you need room to cap off the screws.

3. **Assemble the joint with glue.** If adding screws immediately, you don't even need clamps.

TIP Whenever drilling through a workpiece, it's a good idea to support the back face with a piece of scrap. This helps prevent tearout when the bit plunges through.

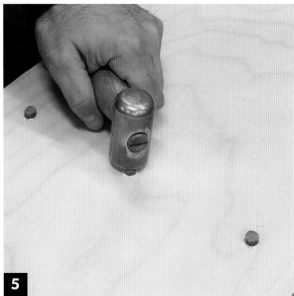

4. Drive screws through the dado and into the adjoining panel. Note that sometimes it's best to drill a pilot hole before driving the screws. This can prevent splitting in the adjoining board.

5. Cut small lengths of dowel rod and glue them into the countersunk hole. Contrasting material can be used for a decorative effect, or face-grain plugs can be cut from the same species in an attempt to hide the reinforcement.

6. Use a flush trim saw to cut the plugs flush with the surface.

7. Sand the surface smooth. The decorative impact of using a contrasting species for the plugs will be even more pronounced once finish is applied.

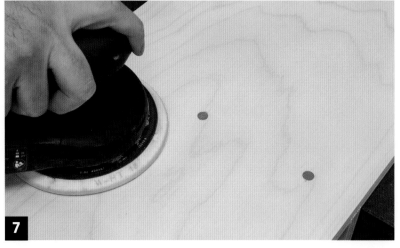

FINESSING THE DEPTH

When cutting rabbets, dadoes, and grooves, it's all too easy to end up with an inconsistent depth from the workpiece lifting, slightly bowed material, or good old human error. Of course we woodworkers never make mistakes, but just in case someone else comes into your shop and puts this flaw into your work, it's good to know how to fix it. Enter the router plane!

1. **Identify the lowest part of** the dado, rabbet, or groove and set the blade to that level.

2. **Push the router plane** forward and it will slice away any material that's higher than the set point. Run the plane from the outside-in at the edges. Make sure the depth is consistent across the entire joint.

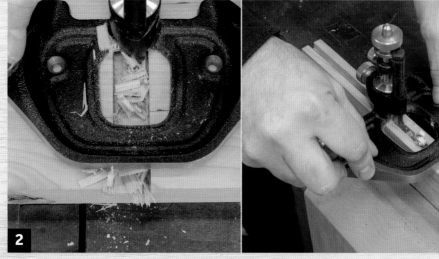

Chapter 3

MORTISES + TENONS

The mortise and tenon is easily the most common structural woodworking joint. By cutting a deep recess in one piece (the mortise) and milling the end of the adjoining piece to the same dimension as the recess (the tenon), we gain an incredible amount of mechanical strength and glue surface when the two are brought together.

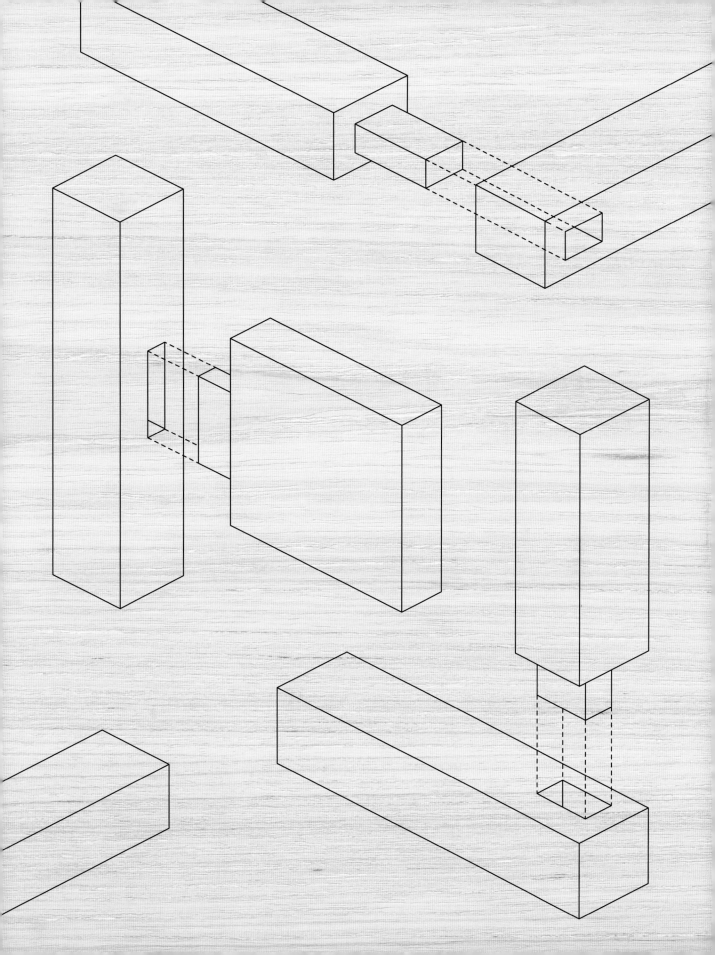

MORTISES

The mortise is the "female" side of the mortise and tenon joint. A recess is cut into the workpiece to accept a tenon. The mortise is typically cut first since the tools used to cut the mortise are of a fixed dimension (e.g., a router bit, drill bit, or chisel).

START *with the* LAYOUT

TOOLS

Adjustable square

1. Mark the length of the mortise at both the beginning and end.

2. Mark the width of the mortise. If the mortise is centered on the thickness of the workpiece, mark in from each face.

Layout should be performed on a workpiece that is milled flat and square. Use an adjustable square and a .5mm mechanical pencil to define the exact location of the mortise.

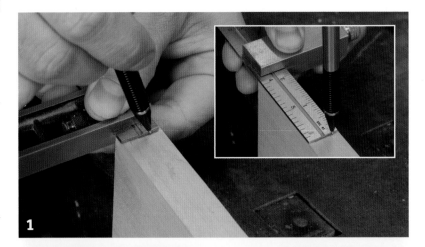

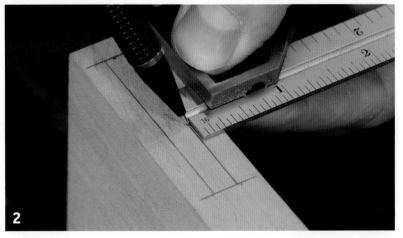

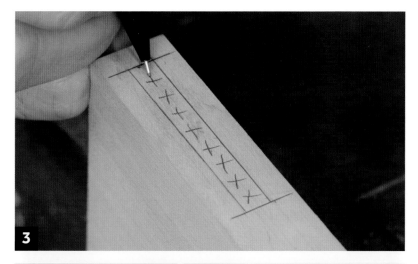

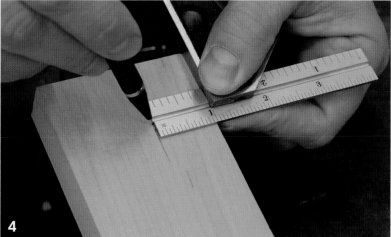

3. It's a good idea to place marks in the mortise area to make it crystal clear where you're supposed to remove material.

4. On the face of the workpiece, mark the depth of the mortise.

5. If laying out multiple workpieces, you only need to do the full layout on one piece. If you use multiple squares for layout, you can easily transfer the start and stop points of the mortise to subsequent pieces. You soon see why this is all you need.

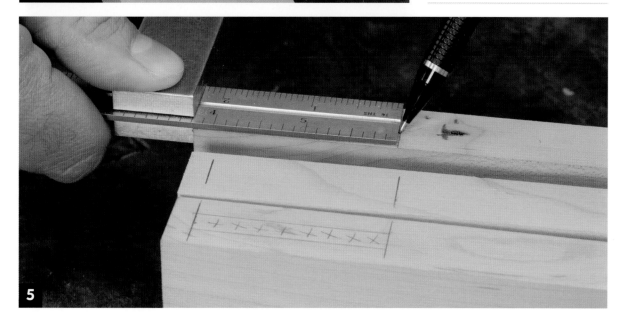

COMMONSENSE MORTISE + TENON SIZING

Mortise and tenon sizing varies depending on the project, the material, and who is making it. There are some traditional rules you can follow, but they get a little confusing and they might give you the wrong impression: that is, if the joint isn't the perfect size, your project will fall apart. Since this book is generally aimed at beginners, here are some basic guidelines in hopes of not bogging you down with details that only result in diminishing gains. Once you understand the joint a little better and you have a few dozen behind you, you should consider taking some time to research traditional mortise and tenon sizing, if only as an academic exercise. For now, let's keep it simple and stick to a commonsense approach. If the tenon looks out of proportion (too long or too thin) or if the mortise looks too substantial (too deep or leaving thin mortise walls), you'll want to make some adjustments.

Tenon Thickness

Make the tenon one-third the thickness of the tenon workpiece if the mortise workpiece is the same thickness. For example, a ¾"-thick workpiece joining another ¾"-thick workpiece would do well with a ¼"-thick tenon. The matching mortise would leave ¼"-thick mortise walls, which are strong enough for most applications. If those walls start to get any thinner, they could be a little too weak.

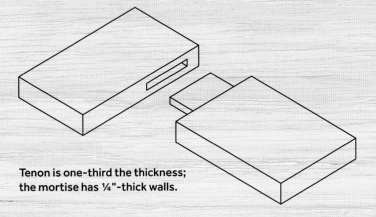

Tenon is one-third the thickness; the mortise has ¼"-thick walls.

Make the tenon thicker if the mortise workpiece is thicker than the tenon piece. For example, if joining a ¾"-thick rail to a 2"-thick table leg, you'd make the tenon ⅜" or ½" thick. Just be sure to have at least a ⅛" shoulder all around the tenon. The 2"-thick leg will have ample material surrounding the mortise.

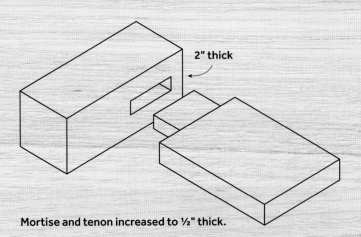

2" thick

Mortise and tenon increased to ½" thick.

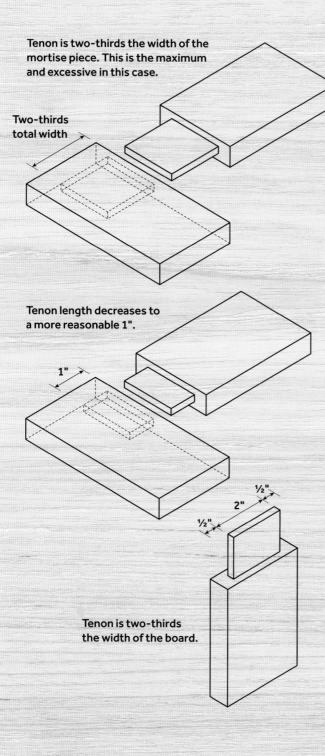

Tenon is two-thirds the width of the mortise piece. This is the maximum and excessive in this case.

Two-thirds total width

Tenon length decreases to a more reasonable 1".

1"

½"

2"

½"

Tenon is two-thirds the width of the board.

Tenon Length

Tenon length can be highly variable; the true limiting factor here is the mortise piece, so think in terms of mortise depth and not necessarily tenon length. You generally don't want mortises to penetrate more than two-thirds of the way through the workpiece. Let's say we're assembling a 3" wide, ¾"-thick door frame. You would make the mortise depth (and tenon length) a maximum of 2". Note, that is the *maximum*. Sprinkle in a dash of common sense and ask yourself if a simple door frame really requires 2"-long tenons. You also might ask if the tools you're using to make the mortise will easily allow cutting of a 2" mortise depth. In most cases, both answers are no. So it's perfectly reasonable to decrease the mortise depth to the 1 to 1¼" range. A mortise of that size is much easier to cut and has plenty of strength for the average door frame.

Tenon Width

Aim for your tenons to be about two-thirds the width of the tenon board. For example, a 3" wide board would have a 2" wide tenon, giving a ¼" shoulder on each side. This rule of thumb works well until you venture into really wide tenons at 4" wide or greater. At that point you'll want to look into splitting the tenon into multiple tenons instead of one large tenon, but that's beyond the scope of this book.

DRILL + CHISEL

TOOLS

Drill press (or drill)
Brad-point drill bit
Chisel
Mallet
Chisel guide
Clamp

The simplest, but certainly not easiest, method for making a mortise involves a drill and a chisel. It is best to use a drill press for the sake of accuracy, but a hand-held drill can work too. The drill bit removes the bulk of the material and the chisel refines the mortise size and shape.

1. Select a drill bit that matches the width of the mortise. A brad-point bit is best because the center spur helps prevent deflection of the bit.

2. At the drill press, set the depth using the depth mark on the face of the board. It's a good idea to let the tips of the bit go just a little below the line.

3. Set up the fence so the bit is centered in the mortise. A featherboard helps yield consistent results.

4. Work from one end to the other, removing the waste. Make sure the bit is fully surrounded by wood each time your drill, otherwise the bit could start to "walk" on you.

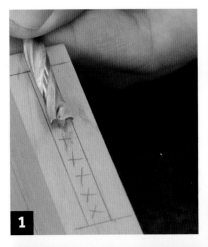

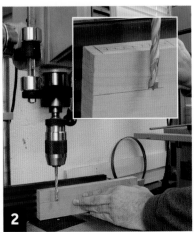

TIP Chiseling perfectly vertical (or perpendicular) to the surface is pretty tricky to do. Err on the side of caution by angling the chisel in slightly, resulting in a mortise that flairs out at the bottom by a fraction of a degree. This helps ensure the tenon won't get caught up on the mortise ends on the way down.

5. **Chisel the ends of the** mortise with the chisel placed directly on the layout lines.

6. **Construct a chisel guide** using quick-drying cyanoacrylate glue. The guide helps keep your chisel aligned when cleaning up the mortise walls.

7. **Clamp the guide to the edge** the workpiece and use it to guide your chisel when you clean up the mortise.

8. Clamp the guide to the chisel workpiece and rest the chisel back against the guide. Chop straight down to clean up the mortise wall, applying consistent pressure against the guide the entire time.

9. Move the guide to the other face and repeat the chiseling process.

10. Use a chisel to remove the any remaining chips that might be left in the mortise and inspect the results. The mortise walls won't be perfectly smooth and they don't need to be.

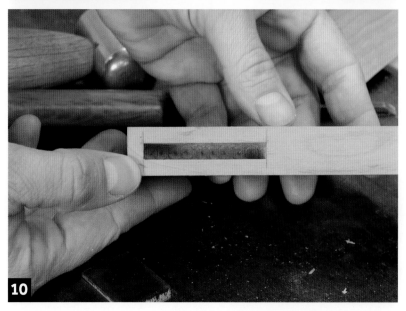

HANDHELD ROUTER + EDGE GUIDE

You just can't beat the versatility of a plunge router outfitted with an edge guide. There are lots of tools and jigs on the market that help you make mortises, but if you master this one technique, you'll always have options even when the jigs and gimmicks fall short.

TOOLS

Adjustable square
Router (plunge preferred)
Edge guide
Straight bit (spiral preferred)

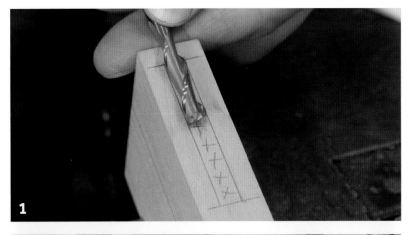

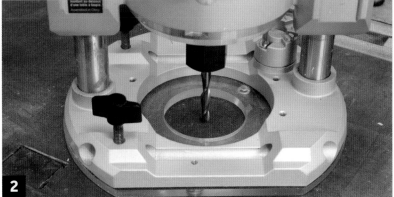

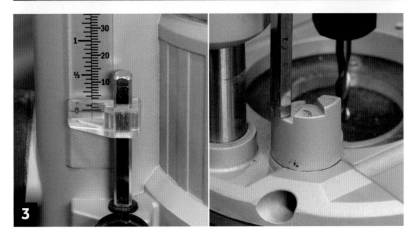

1. **Select a straight bit that** matches the width of the mortise. It is a good idea to invest in a set of up-cut spiral bits for the most common mortise sizes: ¼", ⅜", and ½". Spiral bits are pricier, but they are easier to plunge, cut cleaner, and last longer than regular straight flute bits.

2. **Install the bit and with the** motor off and plunge the bit down until it makes light contact with a flat surface, such as your workbench.

3. **Set the turret stop so the rod** is in contact with the lowest stop and the measurement guide is at zero.

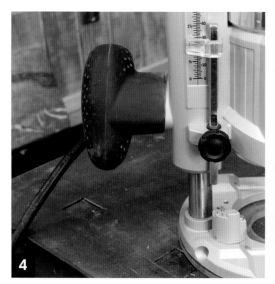

4. Raise the rod to the desired mortise depth and lock it in place. The router is now set to plunge to the desired depth. If the mortise is more than ½" deep, consider rotating the turret stop a couple of times to help facilitate making the mortise in multiple passes.

5. Sandwich the workpiece between two other pieces of stock to create a wider, more stable routing surface. If you're centering the mortise, make sure the support boards are the same thickness.

6. With the edge guide installed, center the bit within the mortise area. Remember to rotate the bit so that the tips of the bit are oriented perpendicular to the mortise. This makes it easier to line up accurately.

7. At one end, plunge to the full depth and raise the bit.

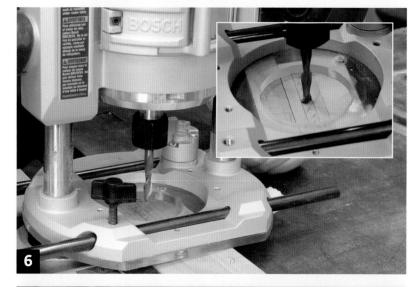

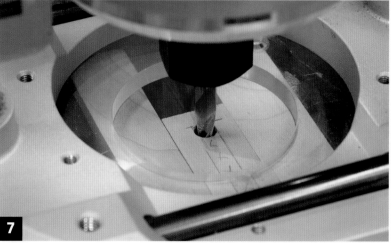

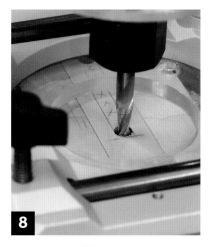

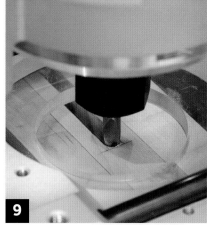

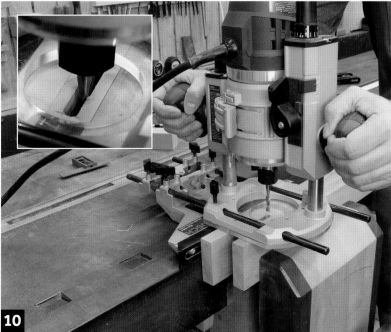

8. Repeat the full plunge at the other end of the mortise to establish the beginning and end of the mortise and provide "safe zones" that can be heard and felt when routing.

9. Route from one end to remove the material between the holes. If the mortise is more than ½" deep, make use of the rotating turret stops to cut in multiple passes.

10. If a centered mortise is required, position the router with the guide on the opposite face and make one full-depth pass. If you have a good eye and centered the bit nicely at the beginning, there won't be much material to remove at this step.

11. The end result will likely be a perfectly centered mortise that is slightly wider than the bit diameter. You haven't made the tenon yet, so that slightly wider mortise won't be a problem.

MAKE A MISPLACED MORTISE DISAPPEAR

There's a reason this book places so much emphasis on joinery layout: no one likes making mistakes. Even with potentially obsessive precautions, anyone can occasionally misplace a mortise either through complacency or a measuring error. In this example, the mortise is just slightly off-target. The fix entails filling the mortise and re-cutting the joint in the proper location.

1. **Cut a patch to fit. This** mortise was cut with a router, so the patch has to have the edges rounded over to match. An end-grain patch is easier to cut, but a long-grain patch will look better. You'll see the long-grain patch in this example.

2. **Insert the patch into the** mortise with glue and tap it home. Once dry, saw off the excess with a flush trim saw and plane or sand the surface flush.

3. **Re-draw the mortise layout** in the proper location and re-cut it. In this case, the tenon shoulder doesn't completely cover the flaw; however this long-grain patch makes the fix very hard to spot.

HOLLOW CHISEL MORTISER

A hollow chisel mortiser is a wonderfully specialized tool that has one job: making mortises. The machine operates much like a drill press. The cutter itself consists of a boring bit surrounded by a square chisel. As the bit creates a round hole, the chisel follows closely behind, transforming the round hole into a square one. This is why mortisers have such large handles: you need the leverage! On the plus side, these tools produce serviceable square-ended mortises fairly quickly. On the minus side, they can be little tricky to calibrate, the mortise walls tend to be fairly rough, and on harder woods, you can be in for quite a workout.

TOOLS

Hollow chisel mortiser
Clamp

1. **Set the plunge depth of the** mortiser using the depth line on the face of the board. It's a good idea to set the chisel so the four tips are below the layout line.

2. **Position the fence so** the chisel is centered in the mortise and set up stop blocks for repeatability, if necessary.

3. **Start at one end of the** mortise and plunge the bit into the workpiece. Allow the tool to clear the chips, but don't go so slowly that it overheats the bit.

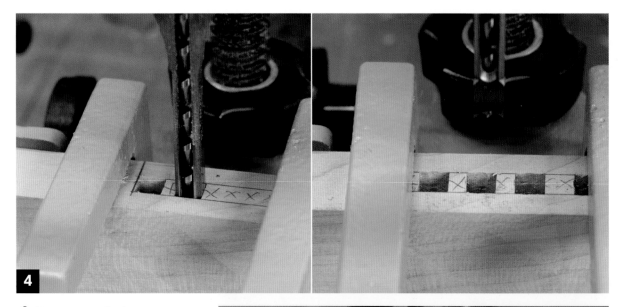

4.

4. Between each plunge, leave a small amount of supporting material. Without wood on all four sides, the bit can skew as it plunges down.

5. Once the end of the mortise is reached, go back and remove the small areas that were previously skipped.

6. The resulting mortise needs very little work once cut. Running a chisel across the bottom to remove the hangers-on is about all it should require.

5.

6.

TENONS

The tenon is the "male" side of the mortise and tenon joint. Material is removed from the end of the workpiece to create a tenon that is sized to fit the adjoining mortise. Tenons are cut in a variety of ways, but they all allow you to sneak up on the perfect fit, which is why the tenon is typically cut after the mortise.

START *with the* LAYOUT

Layout should be performed on a workpiece that is milled flat and square. There are several options for layout tools and your choices will come down to personal preference. Shown here is a cutting gauge with a knife insert to establish the shoulder of the tenon. This cross-grain scribe line not only gives a visual reference for machine setup; it also pre-cuts the grain, resulting in tearout-free cuts. Use an adjustable square and a 5mm mechanical pencil where needed.

TOOLS

Cutting gauge
Adjustable square

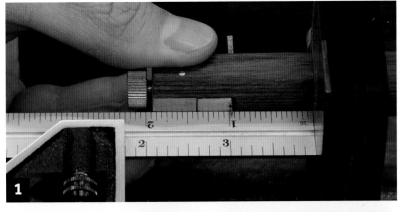

1. **Set up the cutting gauge** for the desired tenon length. To allow room for air and glue in the mortise, make the tenon about $\frac{1}{32}$ to $\frac{1}{16}$" less than the full depth of the mortise.

2. **Mark the shoulders on all** four sides of the board using the cutting gauge.

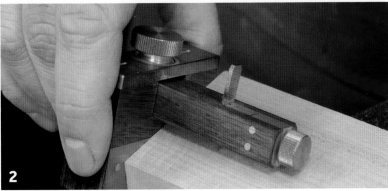

3. **Mark the tenon thickness and** width on the end grain using a pencil and an adjustable square.

4. **Measure twice, cut once.** Since the mortise is already cut, it never hurts to check the tenon layout directly against the mortise.

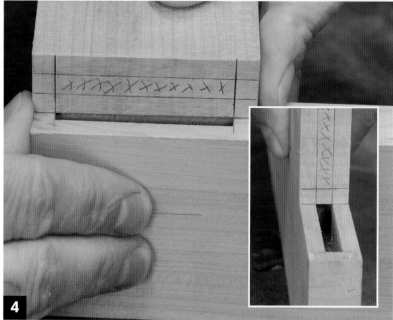

TABLESAW *with* DADO BLADE + MITER GAUGE

Some tablesaws can handle a special cutting blade known as a dado stack. Instead of a single blade, it's a sandwich of blades and chippers that allow you to make much wider cuts than a standard ⅛" kerf blade. Combined with a miter gauge, it's a quick and accurate way to make tenons.

TOOLS

Tablesaw
Dado blade
Miter gauge

1. Set up the dado blade for maximum width, usually ¾ to ⅞".

2. Set the blade height so the teeth are just below the layout line. Shoot for a slightly oversized tenon that allows you to sneak up on the perfect fit.

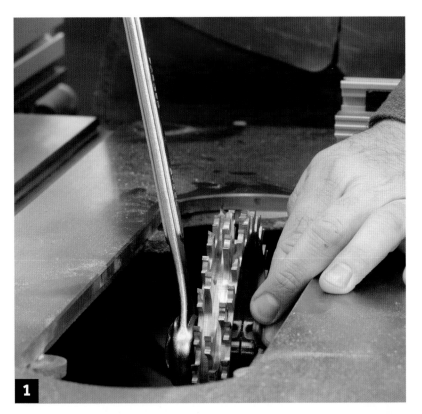

3. With a miter gauge in place, position the tablesaw fence so that the left side of the dado blade just barely touches the shoulder line on the workpiece.

4. Make a test cut on each face, removing only about ⅛" from the front of the workpiece. This is a low-risk way of testing the setup. Even if the tenon is too thin, we're only affecting the first ⅛" and can correct the fit with subsequent cuts.

5. Test the fit with one of the previously cut mortises. The tenon should be just a bit smidge too tight.

6. Raise the blade height slightly and repeat as many times as is necessary to sneak up on the perfect fit (see sidebar, page 114).

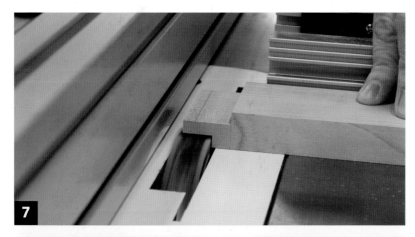

7. With the fit established, cut the remainder of the tenon on both faces, all the way to the shoulder. The fence acts as a stop.

TIP If the long and short shoulders of the tenon are different dimensions, I recommend cutting the tenon cheeks on all of your workpieces first. Only after all the cheeks are cut will I proceed to cutting the short shoulders, as this requires a change in blade height. Remember, it's always best to batch out your parts in order to limit error from setup changes.

8. Cut the short shoulders. In this example, the shoulders are the same on all four sides of the tenon, so no adjustments are needed to the blade height for the short shoulder cuts.

9. When it fits, the mortise should slide in without the need for a mallet.

FINESSING THE FIT

Over the course of cutting multiple tenons on multiple workpieces, inevitably, some will be ever-so-slightly different than the rest. It is wise to err on the side of caution with tenon fit by leaving most pieces a tad snug. This way, you can finesse the perfect fit with hand tools.

1. **To thin down the tenon,** first use a chisel to chamfer the sides of the tenon. This helps prevent blowout from planing.

2. **Take a light pass or two** holding the rabbeting block plane or shoulder plane tight against the tenon shoulder. Be sure to take the same number of passes on each side of the tenon to keep the tenon perfectly centered.

3. **Sometimes, the shoulders** themselves can be a little out of alignment and prevent the joint from seating properly. Use a sharp chisel to pare away any offending material.

4. **Test the fit and repeat the** planing process if needed.

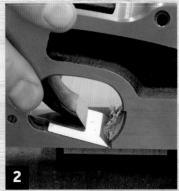

WHAT IS "THE PERFECT FIT"?

I often refer to "the perfect fit" when it comes to joinery, but what exactly does that mean? In my opinion, a perfect-fitting joint is one that goes together by hand and does not require the use of a hammer or mallet to assemble. Once joined, the pieces should not fall apart on their own. We often use the term "friction fit" to describe the ideal situation where friction alone keeps the joint together. Remember, water-based glues swell the wood fibers; if the pieces require a mallet to go together when dry, they will likely be very difficult to assemble when soaked with glue.

ALTERNATIVE METHODS

CLEAN CUTS WITH AN AUXILIARY FENCE

In this book, you'll frequently see use of a cutting gauge to slice across the grain to prevent tearout. Another great trick you should employ is the use of a sacrificial auxiliary fence on the miter gauge. The fence can be made from any flat shop scrap and should extend past the miter fence and into the path of the blade. The fence will then support the fibers in the workpiece as they're being cut, helping prevent tearout.

1. Attach the auxiliary fence using double-stick tape or T-track hardware. With the fence overhanging the blade, a zero clearance opening is established and the wood fibers are supported during the cut.

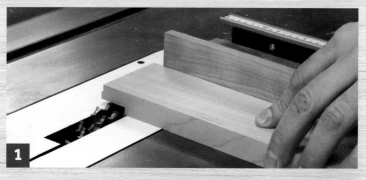

2. The result is a nice clean cut with no tearout. I still scribe my shoulder lines with a cutting gauge. Coupled with an auxiliary fence, it's a bit of a belt and suspenders approach, which is good since I like baggy pants.

TABLESAW *with* TENONING JIG

Tablesaw
Miter gauge
Tenoning jig

A tenoning jig is a device designed to slide back and forth in the miter slot of a tablesaw; it holds workpieces securely in a vertical orientation. The advantage of this is that the tenon cheek is cut quickly and efficiently in a single pass, resulting in an incredibly smooth surface. These jigs also typically feature a micro-adjustment tool, so they are very easy to dial-in to the perfect setting. Thanks to their beefy construction, they produce incredibly consistent results and are the perfect tool when you need to batch out a lot of tenons.

1. **Set the blade height using** the tenon layout on the workpiece. The blade should just touch the pencil line.

2. **With a miter gauge in place,** line up the blade just inside the shoulder layout line. You can use the fence as a stop or if the workpiece is short enough, use the stop included on the miter fence. Make a cut on each face to establish the long shoulders.

3. **Make the short shoulder** cuts, then make an additional series of cuts to nibble away the rest of the tenon width.

4. **Raise the height of the blade** so that it cuts into the shoulder kerf cut that was made in step 3.

5. **Install the workpiece in the** tenoning jig, making sure it is clamped firmly and positioned perfectly perpendicular to the tablesaw surface.

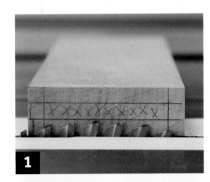

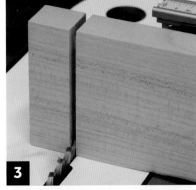

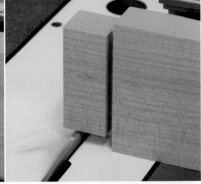

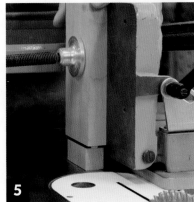

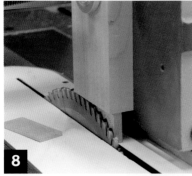

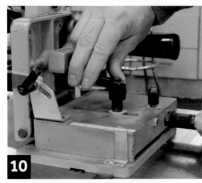

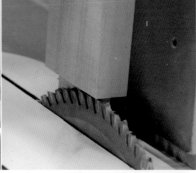

6. Use the adjustments on the jig to move the workpiece over so the blade cuts just outside the tenon layout line. Note that you'll need to redraw these lines after cutting away the short shoulders. The goal is a slightly oversized tenon that allows you to sneak up on the fit.

7. Make the first cheek cut.

8. Flip the piece around and make the second cheek cut.

9. Test the fit with one of the mortises. It should be too thick.

10. Make the fine adjustments needed to push the workpiece ever-so-slightly closer to the blade and repeat the cuts.

11. Repeat as needed until the perfect fit is achieved. This setting can now be used for any other parts that require the same tenon.

BULK UP A TENON CUT TOO THIN

A popular thing to say in woodworking is "You can take wood away but you can't put it back." But is that really true? When I cut a tenon too loose, putting wood back is exactly what I do to fix it! By gluing on thin sheets of scrap stock, I can re-cut the tenon to the perfect size and no one will be the wiser.

1. Glue two thin pieces of scrap to both tenon cheeks.

2. Re-cut the tenon to the perfect size. It doesn't have to be pretty.

3. Once coated with glue and fully inserted into the mortise, the tenon will be perfectly stable and no one will ever see the repair.

ROUTER TABLE

A router table is a compelling choice for making tenons; the bits generally leave a nice clean surface, and the router table offers as much adjustability as a tablesaw.

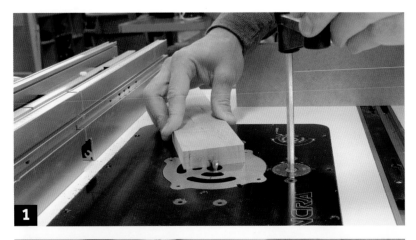

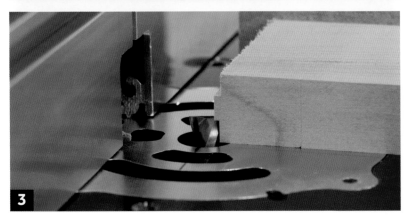

TOOLS

Router table
Straight bit (spiral preferred)

1. Set the bit height so the bit is just under the tenon layout line. The result should be a slightly oversized tenon that will allow you to sneak up on the perfect fit.

2. With the end of the workpiece against the fence, adjust the fence so the wing of the bit just barely touches the shoulder line.

3. Make a test cut on each face, removing only about ⅛" from the end of the workpiece. This is a low-risk way of testing the setup. Even if the tenon is too thin, we can make an adjustment that will correct the fit on the rest of the tenon.

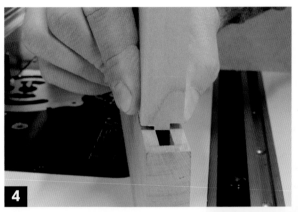

4

5

4. **Test the fit with the** previously cut mortise. The tenon should be too thick.

5. **Raise the bit slightly and** repeat the test cuts until the tenon tip fits into the mortise.

6. **Cut the remainder of the** tenon, working back to the shoulder.

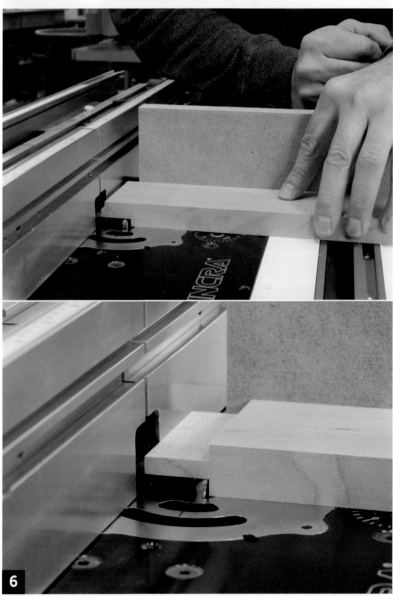

6

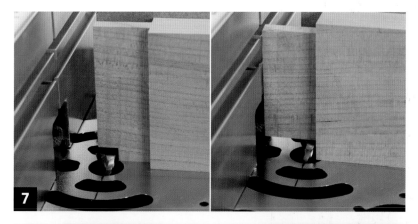

7. **If the short shoulder of the** tenon is a different dimension than the long shoulder, adjust the bit height using the same method shown previously (page 119) and cut the short shoulders. Only do this after the cheek cuts have been made on all workpieces that require this particular tenon.

8. **Test the fit. Aim for a joint** that goes together with only a little hand pressure.

SHOULDER PLANES ARE A JOINER'S SECRET WEAPON

Even if you're exclusively a power tool woodworker, there are some very useful hand tools that can get you out of a bind. When a tenon is just a bit too snug, a quick pass with a shoulder plane can be faster and more accurate than resetting a power tool for another cut. The added bonus is there's almost no risk of removing too much material.

BANDSAW

TOOLS

Bandsaw
Adjustable square
Featherboard
Chisel
Shoulder plane or rabbeting
block plane

The bandsaw is another great tool for making tenons. Lots of folks are moving away from the tablesaw for fear of its powerful kickback potential, and many hand tool–focused shops still have a bandsaw. With the proper setup, it can make quick work of cutting tenons.

1. Calibrate the bandsaw so the blade is running true and the fence is perfectly square to the table and parallel to the blade.

2. Setup should be done using a scrap piece cut to the same thickness as your workpiece. Adjust the fence so the blade cuts just outside the tenon layout line. Use a featherboard to keep the work firmly against the fence.

3. Make the cut to establish the first tenon cheek.

TIP For more on bandsaw tuneup, go to thewoodwhisperer.com/videos/best-way-set-bandsaw

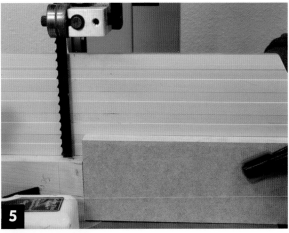

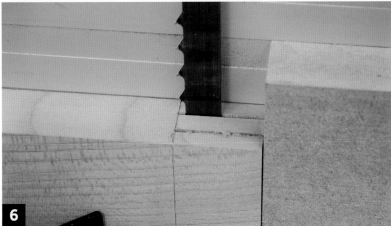

4. When the blade reaches the shoulder scribe line, turn off the saw and hold the workpiece firmly in place while the blade comes to a complete stop.

5. Clamp a piece of scrap to the fence, butted against the workpiece. This will serve as a stop for future cuts.

6. Flip the workpiece and make the second cheek cut.

7. Expose the tenon by cutting the ends off without cutting into the tenon itself.

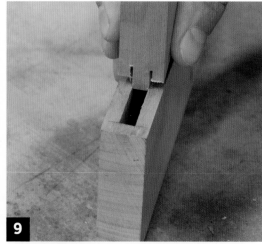

8. Test the fit with the previously cut mortise and adjust the fence position if needed. In this example, the tenon is too thin. Good thing this is just a test piece.

9. Use the opposite end of the test piece to repeat the process. If another adjustment is needed, cut the ends off the test piece and try again.

10. Once dialed in, make the cheek cuts on the actual workpieces.

11. To cut the tenon to width, adjust the fence to the appropriate position and make both cuts. If the long and short shoulders are the same dimension, you shouldn't need to move the fence at all.

12. To cut the shoulders, install a miter gauge and set the fence so the blade cuts just inside the shoulder scribe line.

13. Cut the shoulders on all four sides of the board. Keep in mind there is no depth stop being shown for the sake of simplicity. When the cut piece falls off, the cut is complete.

14. Bandsawn tenons often require cleanup at the workbench. Remove any proud material from the short shoulders using a chisel.

15. The long shoulders can be finessed with a shoulder plane, bringing them in line (coplanar) with one another. A slight chamfer cut on the edge helps prevent tearout.

16. **If the tenon is a bit snug,** finesse the cheeks with a shoulder plane or rabbeting block plane.

17. **Remember to chamfer the** corner to avoid tearout.

18. **Insert the tenon into the** mortise and make further adjustments if necessary.

ROUNDING *the* TENON

So far, every tenon in this book has had square sides. You might recall that mortises cut with a router have round ends due to the shape of a router bit. Since a square peg obviously can't fit into a round hole, what can be done? Though you could square the mortise using a chisel, it is a little time consuming and less fun than the method shown here: rounding the tenon.

TOOLS
Rasp
Chisel

1. **Using a small rasp, round over** the corners manually until they roughly match the round shape of the mortise.

2. **The rasp could easily damage** the tenon shoulder, so, using a chisel, sever the fibers at the base of the tenon.

3. **Carefully chop down to** finalize the shape of the base of the tenon.

4. **Test the fit and refine if** needed. A well-fitted tenon should slide smoothly into place with only a little hand pressure.

LOOSE MORTISE + TENON

The tenons cut so far are known as *integral tenons*, meaning they are directly attached to the tenon workpiece. An alternative version of the classic mortise and tenon joint is the loose (or floating) mortise and tenon. Both workpieces receive a mortise and a tenon is cut as a separate component.

MORTISE *with* ROUTER + EDGE GUIDE

TOOLS

Cutting gauge
Adjustable square
Router with edge guide
Clamps

1. Lay out the mortise on the end grain of the workpiece and clamp it in a vertical position to the workbench.

2. Attach two flat and straight pieces of stock (plywood and MDF work great) perpendicular to the workpiece and flush with the end grain. This setup will provide the necessary support for the router.

The mortises for a loose mortise and tenon joint are cut in the same manner as described in the beginning of this chapter. The only difference is with reference to the workpiece that would traditionally receive the tenon.

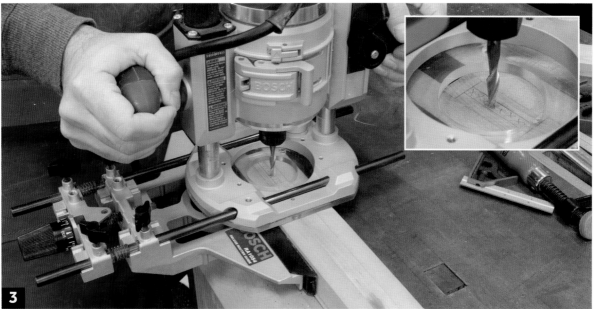

3

4

3. With the edge guide installed, position the bit so it's centered with the mortise area.

4. The adjoining piece receives a mortise that is cut exactly as described previously (page 104).

LOOSE TENONS

TOOLS

Featherboard
Bandsaw or tablesaw
Handplane or router with
roundover bit

1. **Cut a tenon strip to rough** thickness at the bandsaw or tablesaw. The width of the strip should be oversized at this stage.

2. **A handplane is great for** smoothing the surface left by the bandsaw and also allows you to easily sneak up on the perfect fit.

3. **Test the fit in one of the** mortises and reduce the thickness as needed.

The best part of loose mortise and tenon joinery is that making the tenon stock is a completely separate step, rather than fussing with the size of a tenon on the end of a workpiece. It is a good idea to make loose tenons from project scrap of the same species.

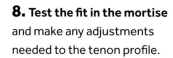

4. **With the tenon in the** mortise, mark the width.

5. **Cut the tenon strip to the** layout line at the tablesaw or bandsaw.

6. **Round over the edges of the** tenon strip using a handplane. It's not critical to match the profile of the mortise perfectly.

7. **If you have a lot of tenons to** round, a roundover bit and a router provide excellent results.

8. **Test the fit in the mortise** and make any adjustments needed to the tenon profile.

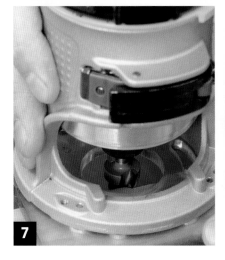

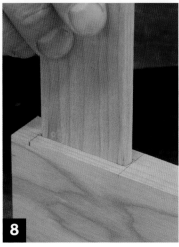

9. Cut the tenon strip into individual tenons of the appropriate length. Remember to cut them about 1/32 to 1/16" shy of the total mortise depth, allowing for air and glue.

10. Test assemble. Just be careful; these tenons often fit so snugly that they are difficult to remove.

11. To glue up, apply glue to the mortises and spread it evenly.

12. Brush glue onto the tenon in a thin layer to prevent excessive squeeze-out when the joint goes together.

13. Bring it all together. If your dry-fit went smoothly, glue-up should as well.

FESTOOL DOMINO

In 2007, Festool released a new joinery tool called the Domino Joiner. There's no arguing with the fact that it is one of the few true game-changers to arrive in the modern woodworking world. The tool can cut perfect mortises in seconds, thanks to a rotating and oscillating cutter. Festool also sells premade Domino tenons sized perfectly for various cutter sizes and depth settings. For those who have the budget to afford one, using the Domino can mean woodworking in easy mode.

But while the Domino is an excellent time-saver for the seasoned woodworker, I often recommend against it for beginners. The skills required to cut a mortise and tenon joint will serve a woodworker well in all aspects of the craft. If you acquire a Domino too early, you may rob yourself of the opportunity to learn these valuable skills. I also often see woodworkers choose a Domino joint for convenience when it is neither the size nor shape that should be used. Of course, these skills can be obtained through other means, so to each his or her own.

TOOLS

Domino joiner
Clamps

---

1. **The Domino comes in two** sizes: Domino 500 and Domino XL.

2. **Making a mortise is a "point** and shoot" activity, not unlike plunging a biscuit joiner.

3. **Once a mortise is cut** into both workpieces, the appropriate Domino tenon can be glued into place.

ANGLED LOOSE MORTISE + TENON

Angled mortise and tenon joints can be quite intimidating. In fact, I used to avoid them at all costs, until I realized how easy they can be when made using loose mortise and tenon construction. Angled mortise and tenons are most common in chairs, but you'll also find them in many other furniture pieces.

MITERED ANGLED MORTISE + TENON

TOOLS

Adjustable square
Tablesaw
Miter gauge
Router
Straight bit (spiral preferred)
Clamp

Angled joints can be somewhat abstract without a frame of reference in an actual project. Pictured below is a simple bench with legs splayed out at an angle. This design requires an angled mortise and tenon joint between the front and rear aprons and the legs. Shown here is a demonstration of how to make the angled joint.

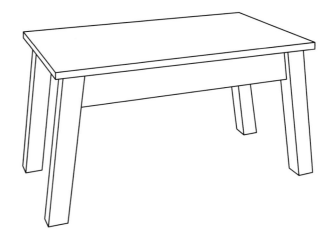

1. Mill the angled piece to size and cut the desired angle on the end using the miter gauge at the tablesaw.

2. The leg will require the same miter angle at both the top and bottom of the leg.

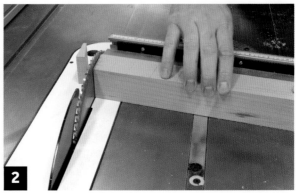

3. Lay out the mortises in both leg and the apron.

4. Draw the mortise depth on both pieces just to confirm the mortise doesn't venture too close to any particular edge.

5. Sandwich the leg between two straight and flat pieces of stock to provide additional support for the router.

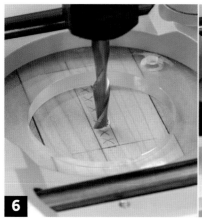  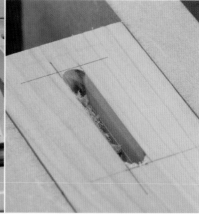

6

6. With the edge guide installed, position the bit so it's centered within the mortise area. Plunge to full depth at the beginning and end of the mortise, then remove the material between the holes in several passes (see pages 104 and 105 for more detail).

7. Mount the mitered apron vertically in the vise on your workbench.

8. Clamp two flat and straight support pieces to the workpiece so they are flush with the mitered end. Using a piece of scrap on top helps keep everything flush while clamping pressure is applied.

7

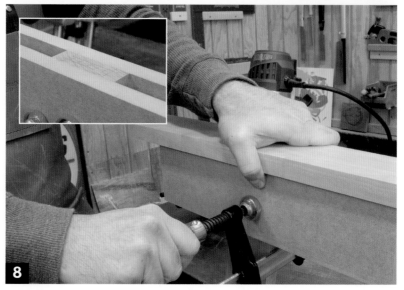

8

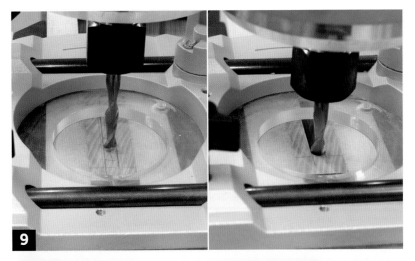

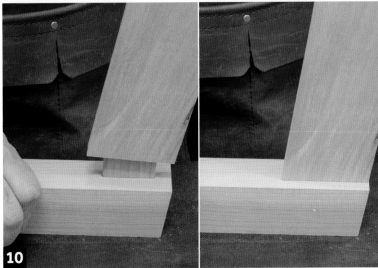

9. **With the edge guide installed,** position the bit so it's centered with the mortise area, plunge to full depth at each end, then clear the material in-between.

10. **Construct the loose tenon** stock as shown on pages 130 to 132. Once cut to size, test the fit.

11. **For the glue-up, it's a good** idea to utilize an angled caul, cut to 10°, to help keep the clamp from denting and slipping.

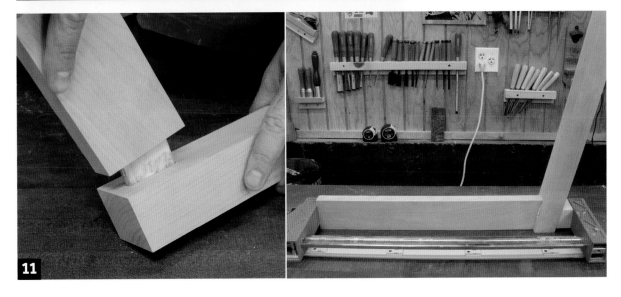

BEVELED ANGLED MORTISE + TENON

TOOLS

Adjustable square
Featherboard
Tablesaw
Miter gauge
Router
Straight bit (spiral preferred)
Clamp

The beveled angled mortise and tenon joint is another joint commonly found in chairs. Chairs often have a trapezoidal shape where legs and rails meet; that joint is accomplished via a beveled angled mortise and tenon. Once again, the loose mortise and tenon construction method make the process much easier than you might think.

1. Bevel the tablesaw blade to the appropriate angle and cut the workpiece to length with a miter gauge.

2. Keep the saw blade at the same angle and rip one edge of two pieces of flat, straight scrap.

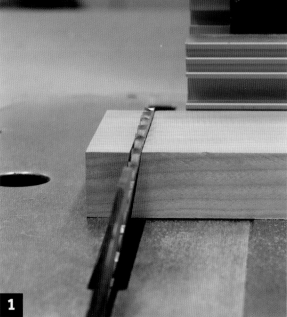

3. Lay out the mortise locations on the rail and leg.

4. With the rail piece clamped vertically, clamp the two angled scrap pieces so the angles all line up and are perfectly flush, providing the additional support the router needs for a safe cut.

5. Set up the router with the edge guide on the uphill side; let gravity work in your favor. Line the bit up with the layout lines and cut the mortise as described on page 137.

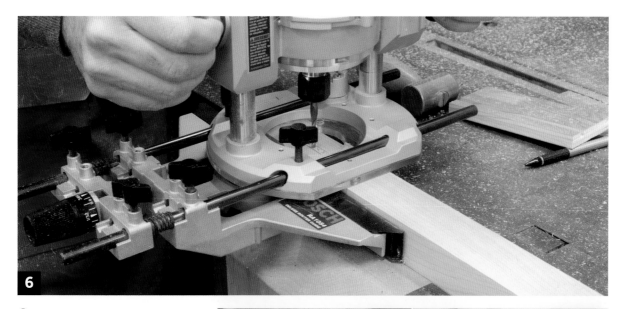

6. **Cut the mortise in the leg as** described on page 137. In this case, the leg is wide enough that it doesn't require additional support for the router.

7. **Construct loose tenon stock** as shown on pages 130 to 132. Once cut to size, test the fit.

8. **When it comes time to glue** up, make use of an angled caul to help stabilize the clamp and prevent slipping.

THROUGH-MORTISE + TENON

Most mortise and tenon joints are hidden after assembly. On occasion, a project will call for a through-mortise and tenon, where the tenon pushes completely through the adjoining workpiece and is visible from the other side. That's when you can show off a little.

THROUGH-MORTISE *in* THIN WORKPIECE

If the piece receiving the through-mortise is thin (less than 1"), the mortise can be routed in one full-depth pass, keeping the mortise walls clean and consistent. To guide the router, use an edge guide and layout lines.

TOOLS

Adjustable square
Router with edge guide
Straight router bit
Clamps
Chisel
Mallet

1. **Lay out the mortise** completely. Pictured are both the thin and thick examples. Let's start with the thin version.

2. **Clamp the show face (the** side that will show the tip of the tenon after assembly) down to the workbench with a sacrificial board underneath.

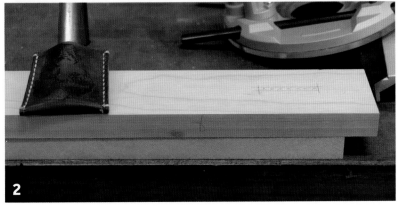

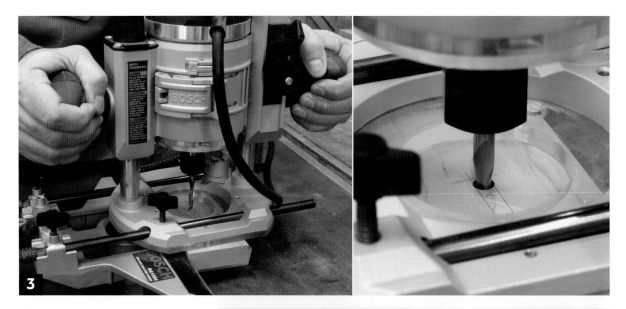

3. Using an edge guide, center the bit in the layout lines and cut the mortise in multiple passes until the bit cuts into the sacrificial backer piece.

4. The backer piece supports the fibers during the cut and leaves a clean, crisp edge.

5. Square up the ends of the mortise carefully by chiseling in from the show face. Use a square to orient the chisel and use hand pressure to press the chisel firmly on the layout line. This should provide enough of a divot to keep the chisel in position even after the square is removed.

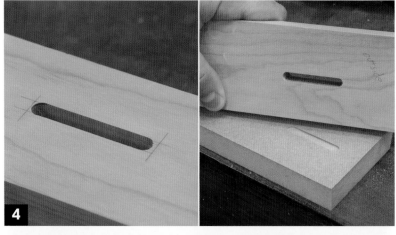

6. **Using a mallet, tap the chisel** and chop the mortise square.

7. **Angle the chisel inward ever-**so-slightly so the entry side of the mortise (the non-show face) becomes slightly wider than the show side. This will make it much easier to install the tenon later.

8. **Use a wide chisel to finish** squaring up the ends by referencing the chisel back against the mortise walls. It shouldn't require more than a little hand pressure to square up the corners.

THROUGH-MORTISE *in* THICK WORKPIECE

TOOLS

Square
Router with edge guide
Router bit (spiral preferred)
Chisel
Mallet

1. To help keep the mortise on track, attach a second fence using double-stick tape. The fence is just a straight piece of scrap.

2. With the router bit aligned over the mortise, the second fence is attached to the base for a snug fit.

3. Double-stick tape is pressure-sensitive, so be sure to give it a good squeeze once the position is established.

4. Route the mortise at least halfway through the workpiece.

If the piece is thicker than 1″, the mortise is usually cut from both faces; the bit is likely too short to make the cut from only one side.

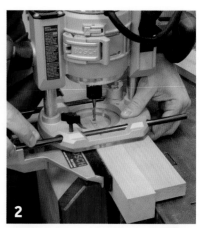

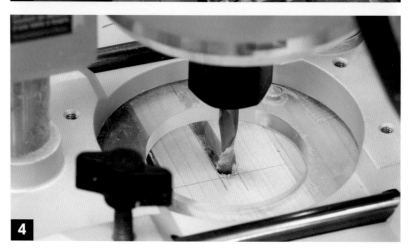

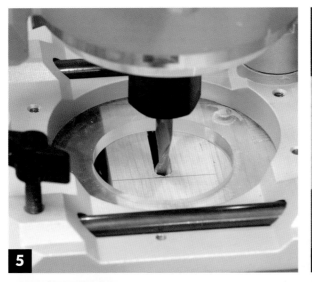

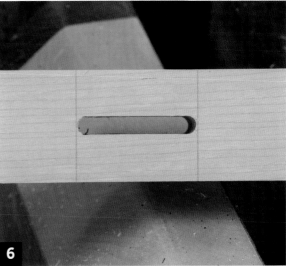

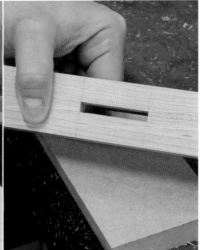

5. Flip the workpiece over and route the mortise in the opposite face, making sure the edge guide references from the same face as in the previous cut. This is critical!

6. The mortise should have clean and consistent walls with no major ridges. If necessary, clean the walls with a wide chisel.

7. Square up the ends using a chisel and a square for alignment.

8. Cut the tenon using your method of choice. The tenon length can be exactly the thickness of the mortise piece for a flush through tenon, or it can be slightly longer for a proud through tenon. Carefully insert the tenon into the mortise to test the fit. Keep test fits to a minimum to avoid damaging the show face of the mortise.

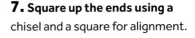

ASSEMBLING *the* JOINT | GLUING *a* THROUGH-MORTISE + TENON

1. To glue up a through tenon, coat the bottom ¾" of the tenon with glue. Do not put any glue on the tip of the tenon or in the mortise.

2. Carefully insert the tenon into the mortise. It may appear to scrape off all of the glue, but there's plenty on the joint.

3. When the tenon protrudes from the other side, there should be no glue to clean up. If you're concerned about not having enough glue coverage, you can assemble the joint with glue on the entire tenon and in the mortise. Just plan on doing a thorough cleanup and subsequent sanding on the other end to prevent discoloration from absorbed glue.

Usually it's fine to be fairly liberal with glue. The mortise and tenon should both receive glue; what isn't absorbed by the joint gets squeezed out. In the case of a through-mortise and tenon, where the tenon tip sits proud of the surface, it pays to a little more judicious.

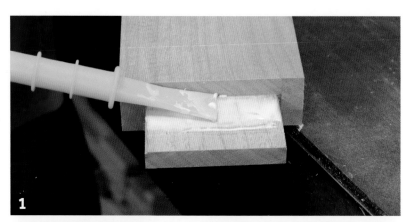

MORTISE *with* TEMPLATE

When the through-mortise is wider than the router bit or when the mortise is located too far from the edge to effectively use an edge guide, the simplicity and repeatability of a routing template and guide bushing setup is handy.

Most routers have bases available that will accept standard guide bushings. The idea behind the guide bushing is that it limits the travel of the router bit within a template. The bit never makes direct contact with the template, allowing the template to be used indefinitely.

TOOLS

Template
Adjustable square
Router
Straight bit (spiral preferred)
Chisel
Mallet

1. **Construct a template from** ½" MDF or plywood. This is thick enough to accommodate the length of most guide bushings, yet thin enough to allow a typical router bit to cut deep enough into the mortise workpiece.

2. **Calculate the offset of the** guide bushing by measuring the distance between the outside of the bit and the outside of the guide bushing. In this example, the distance is ⅛". This means that the hole in the router template needs to be the desired mortise dimension plus ⅛" on all four sides. If the desired mortise is 1½ x 1½", the hole in the jig should be 1¾ x 1¾".

3. Glue the four template pieces together to create the desired size hole after ripping the interior two pieces to the desired width. The pieces should provide enough surface area for not only the router, but also some clamps.

4. When the router sits on the template, the router bit can extend past the template and into the workpiece.

5. **With the template clamped** to the work surface and the show face of the workpiece facing down on a sacrificial board, begin routing the mortise.

6. **Make the mortise in two to** three depth passes, working clockwise around the hole until contact is made with the backer board.

7. **After routing you should**
see a small amount of fuzz on the
non-show face. The show face
should be crisp and clean.

8. **Square the mortise corners**
using a large chisel and chiseling
in from the show face. This
helps prevent damaging the final
appearance of the through tenon.

9. **Prepare the tenon by laying**
out the end grain and shoulders.

10. **Cut the tenon using your**
preferred method.

11. **Test fit and assemble.**

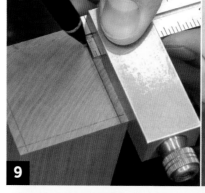

EXTRA-LARGE THROUGH-MORTISES

In some cases, the mortise is so large that you can employ a nifty trick where half of the mortise is cut into two separate pieces. When the pieces are glued together, the full-size mortise is revealed. This technique works well for large tables and workbenches.

TOOLS

Adjustable square
Tablesaw
Dado blade
Miter gauge

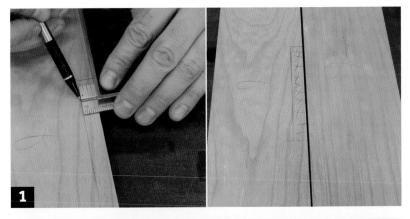

1. **Lay out one half of the** mortise on one workpiece. The other piece can simply receive a few rough reference marks to help orient it later when making the cuts.

2. **At the tablesaw, set up the** dado blade for the widest cut and raise the blade so it's just under the layout lines on the workpiece.

3. **With the miter gauge** installed, set up a two-stop system with the tablesaw fence serving as one stop and the miter gauge stop serving as the other. Use the layout lines as a guide.

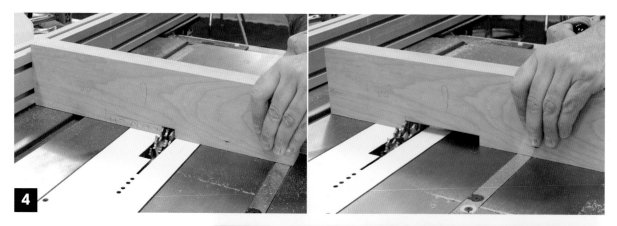

4. Cut the half-mortise, making multiple passes and working from one stop to the other. Repeat the cut on the adjoining workpiece.

5. Glue the two halves back together, making sure the mortise walls are nice and even.

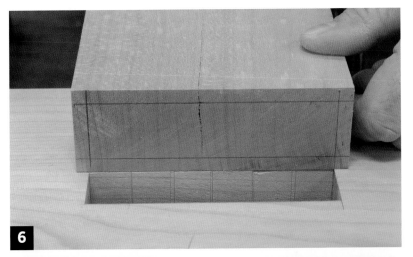

6. Lay out the tenon and double-check the marks against the actual mortise.

7. Cut the tenon using your preferred method. Take your time and slowly sneak up on the fit. The quality of the fit is not only visible in the final product, but usually a visual focal point.

TIP Dado blades tend to leave cross-grain lines in the surface of the tenon. When making a long through tenon, those lines might be visible. It's a good idea to keep your tenon slightly oversized and use a shoulder plane or rabbeting block plane to smooth the cheeks, bringing the tenon down to final size and removing the lines.

Chapter 4

HALF-LAPS + BRIDLES

Half-laps and bridle joints are very similar to mortise and tenon joints. A half-lap joint is made from what are essentially two tenons that each have only one face. The two tenons simply overlap to create a joint. Bridle joints consist of a tenon that is the full width and depth of the workpiece and a mortise that is open on three sides. When the joints close up, both half-laps and bridle joints showcase exposed joinery that lends visual interest to whatever you're building.

While half-laps don't boast the strength of a traditional mortise and tenon joint, they are plenty strong for cabinet frames and small doors. Bridle joints are used in frames and doors of all kinds, and allow the viewer to see exactly how the joint goes together. As far as construction goes, if you can cut a mortise and tenon joint, cutting half-lap or bridle joints requires only a few tweaks to the process.

HALF-LAP CORNER JOINTS

The corner half-lap is commonly used in frame and door construction, many times as an alternative to miter joints or traditional mortise and tenon joints.

TABLESAW *with* DADO STACK + MITER GAUGE

TOOLS

Adjustable square
Cutting gauge
Tablesaw
Dado blade
Miter gauge
Clamps
Handplane

My preferred method for making half-lap joints is with a tablesaw, dado blade, and miter gauge. It's a convenient, quick, and repeatable method that delivers clean results. In this example, the two workpieces being joined are the same width.

1. Set the cutting gauge to the width of workpiece. A trick is setting the gauge slightly less than the width of the workpiece (maybe $\frac{1}{32}$"). This leaves extra material that will come in handy later.

2. Scribe the shoulder on workpiece B using a cutting gauge. If your workpieces are the same width, use this setting to mark the shoulder on workpiece A. If the pieces being joined are different widths, set the gauge to the width of workpiece B and use that setting to mark the shoulder of workpiece A. Mark each board width on its adjoining partner.

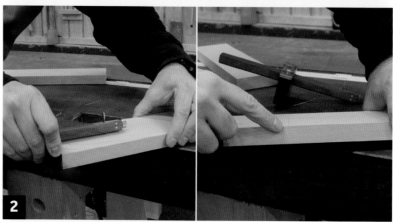

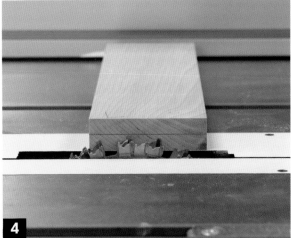

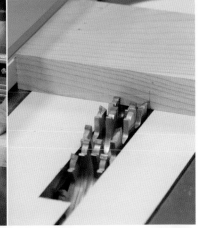

3. **Mark a pencil line halfway** through the thickness of one of the boards.

4. **With the dado blade installed** in the tablesaw and set to maximum width, raise the blade height to just under the pencil line.

5. **With the miter gauge in place,** set the dado blade so the left-most tooth just barely touches the shoulder scribe line.

6. **Cut the half-laps on both** adjoining pieces.

7. Test fit. If you intentionally leave extra material on the joint, you can slowly sneak up on the perfect fit.

8. Raise the blade slightly, cut again, and test fit. Remember, any change you make to the blade height is effectively doubled since the cut is made on both pieces. When the pieces are flush with one another you can cut the remainder of your workpieces.

9. To assemble the joint, apply glue to both half-lap cheeks and shoulders.

10. Apply clamping pressure in both directions to fully seat the joint against the shoulders. You should see a little bit of glue squeeze-out.

11. **Apply clamping pressure to** the face of the joint. A small caul is helpful for spreading out the clamping pressure.

12. **Remember the ⅟₃₂" trick** mentioned in step 1? This is where it pays off. That small amount of material sitting proud of the joint gives our clamp something to press against to close up the shoulder. If that material isn't there, the clamp will press against both workpieces and isn't guaranteed to close up the shoulder without the aid of a small caul.

13. **After the glue dries, if you** employed the trick, use a handplane to remove the ⅟₃₂" excess material and flush it up to the end grain of the joint.

CUTTING A HALF-LAP CORNER JOINT

There are numerous other methods you can use to produce a corner half-lap joint depending on your available tools and personal preferences. Here are a few examples.

Miter Gauge at the Router Table

Making a half-lap at the router table is conceptually the same as the tablesaw, only a straight router bit handles the stock removal. The result is a very smooth cheek and a clean shoulder, provided you scribe the shoulder with a cutting gauge and use an auxiliary fence.

Set the bit height to the half-thickness layout line and the fence to the shoulder layout line. Then remove the stock in multiple passes until the shoulder is reached.

Bandsaw

With a sharp blade and proper calibration, the bandsaw can be used to create serviceable corner half-laps.

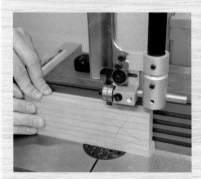
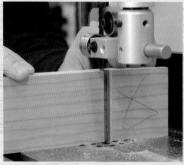

With the blade lined up just inside the layout line and against the fence, make the cut stopping short of the shoulder layout line.

Carefully cut the shoulder along the layout line. A miter gauge can be helpful when making this cut.

The bandsaw tends to leave a rough surface, so consider cleaning up the surface with a shoulder plane or rabbeting block plane (see sidebar on page 121).

Tablesaw with Single Blade + Tenon Jig

With a miter gauge and a stop, cut the shoulder line of the half-lap. Position the workpiece vertically in a tenoning jig and raise the blade so it's just shy of the shoulder. Position the tenoning jig so the blade cuts at the halfway point of the board's thickness and cut the cheek.

Cut the shoulder using a miter gauge.

Cut the tenon using a miter gauge.

Tablesaw with Single Blade + Tall Fence

This method is a lot like using a tenoning jig, only you use a tall fence, a backer board, and a featherboard to keep the vertical workpiece stable. A piece of masking tape further secures the workpiece to the backer board. While this is certainly a viable method, it's by no means a favorite of mine since the workpiece isn't quite as stable as I'd like.

Use a miter gauge to cut the shoulder on the joint.

Carefully make the cheek cut.

Tablesaw with Single Blade

This is probably the most "no frills" method for making the half-lap. Simply make repeated cuts at the tablesaw using a single blade, slowly nibbling away the material. The end result is usually a pretty rough surface that will likely need some finessing at the workbench thanks to the typical alternating bevel design of most tablesaw blades.

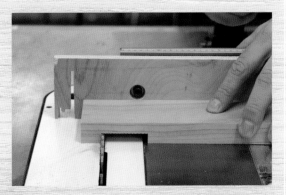

Nibble away the stock using a single blade.

T-SHAPED HALF-LAP

The *T*-shaped half-lap is commonly used in frame construction or any time a divider is needed. Just like a corner half-lap, the joint is deceivingly strong, thanks to the ample glue surface.

TABLESAW *with* DADO STACK + MITER GAUGE

TOOLS

Marking knife
Clamp
Tablesaw
Dado blade
Miter gauge

The dado blade is used to hog away the material on both workpieces, but you must pay special attention to how the half-lap is cut in the middle of the second board.

1. After cutting a single half-lap as described on pages 156 to 158, clamp the half-lap directly to the adjoining board in the desired location. Be sure the shoulder is tight against the workpiece.

2. Use a knife to mark the edges of the half-lap onto the adjoining board. In general, knife lines are more accurate than pencil lines and in this case, you need as much accuracy as you can get.

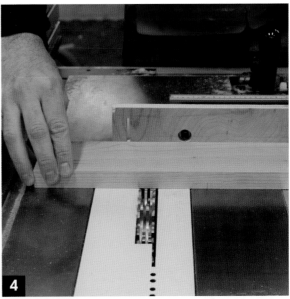

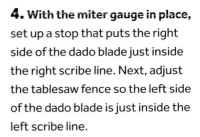

3. Since you already cut the first half-lap, the tablesaw should be set up with the dado blade at the proper height.

4. With the miter gauge in place, set up a stop that puts the right side of the dado blade just inside the right scribe line. Next, adjust the tablesaw fence so the left side of the dado blade is just inside the left scribe line.

5. Cut the half-lap by taking multiple passes.

6. Test the fit by flipping the previously half-lapped workpiece upside down and dropping it between the shoulders of the workpiece.

7. If the fit is too snug (as it should be), adjust one or both stop blocks to widen the half-lap and cut again.

8. Once the perfect fit is achieved, the joint can be glued together with glue on the cheeks and shoulders with clamping pressure to close the shoulders and sandwich the joint together.

ALTERNATIVE METHODS

CUTTING A *T*-SHAPED HALF-LAP

Tablesaw with Single Blade

Using a miter gauge and the dual stop block setup, a single blade can be used to create the half-lap. Simply nibble away the stock from one shoulder to the other. The resulting surface will be a little rough and could benefit from a pass or two of a shoulder plane or rabbeting block plane.

Router Table with Miter Gauge

With a nice sharp straight bit, a miter gauge with an auxiliary fence, and a dual stop setup, the router table is also an effective tool for making the second half of the T-shaped half-lap.

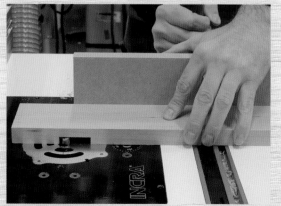

CROSS HALF-LAP

A cross half-lap is used in cases where stock meets in an *X* instead of a *T,* as is often the case on face frames used in cabinetry.

TABLESAW, DADO STACK + MITER GAUGE

If you don't have a dado blade or prefer not to use the tablesaw, the second half of a *T*-shaped half-lap joint can be cut via two alternative methods.

TOOLS

Square
Marking knife
Clamp
Tablesaw
Dado blade
Miter gauge

1. Clamp the two adjoining workpieces together in the desired overlap location and mark the intersections with a marking knife. Be sure to mark the shoulders on the edges as well.

2. Use a fine pencil to reinforce the cut lines, making them easier to see during setup.

3. Mark the faces of each workpiece to indicate where the cuts will occur to prevent confusion.

4. On a piece of scrap milled to the same thickness as our workpieces, mark a half-thickness line and raise the dado blade to just under that line.

5. Make test cuts on the ends of two pieces of scrap to dial in the height setting of the dado blade, essentially creating a corner half-lap.

6. Once the scrap pieces are flush with one another, you know you have the correct blade height setting.

7. Register the stock against the fence and use the miter gauge to push it through the dado blade.

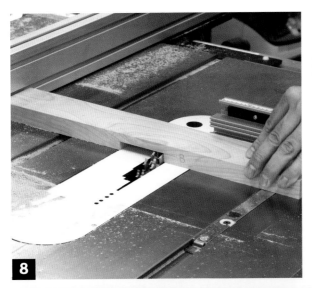

8. Cut the half-lap by taking multiple passes, adjusting the fence as needed and using the miter gauge to keep the cut square.

9. If your adjoining workpiece is the same length and the half-lap is in the same location along the length, you can use the current setup to cut the half-lap. If that's not the case, you'll want to repeat the stop block setup process using the layout lines as a guide.

10. When it's time for glue-up, apply glue to both surfaces and clamp together securely.

11. The only clamp needed for a is cross half-lap is one that presses the faces of the joint together.

CLEANUP + FINESSING

While many of us strive for perfection in woodworking, we have to accept that perfection is a moving target. I mean that literally, since wood is constantly moving due to humidity. Wood also has a tendency to move when cut as pressure is released. As a result, some joints will require just a little more love at the workbench to achieve the "perfect" fit you're after.

Half-laps and tenons typically have milling marks on the surface. A shoulder or rabbeting block plane can be helpful for smoothing them out and thinning the half-lap for the perfect fit.

While a shoulder plane can work on cross and *T*-shaped half-laps, the router plane is usually a better choice. A favorite feature of the router plane is the blade's fixed depth. Once dialed in, you can use that same setting on all of your workpieces for absolute consistency.

CORNER BRIDLE

The corner bridle joint is very similar to a mortise and tenon, except one side of the mortise is open. It creates an exposed joint that not only lends visual interest, but also shows at a glance that the furniture was made with care.

TABLESAW, SINGLE BLADE + TENONING JIG

The "female" side of the corner bridle joint presents a challenge in that it can be difficult to finesse after the cut. Shown here is a method for cutting them with the tablesaw with a dado stack and a tenoning jig. The inner cheeks and the shoulder will be perfectly smooth after the cut.

TOOLS

Marking gauge
Adjustable square
Tablesaw
Tenoning jig
Chisel
Mallet
Clamps

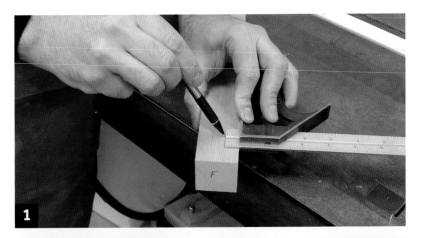

1. **Lay out the female portion of** the joint starting with the spacing. Usually, the width is divided into equal thirds with the center section marked as waste.

2. **Set a marking gauge to the** width of the male workpiece.

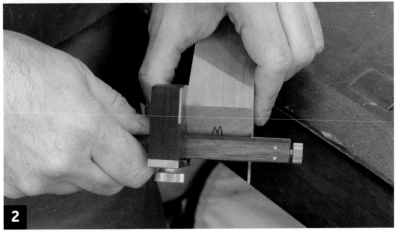

3. Scribe the shoulder on the female workpiece, cutting only between the pencil lines.

4. Use the same gauge setting to scribe the shoulders on the male workpiece.

5. Set the blade height so that it's just under the scribe line on the female workpiece.

6. Line up the tenoning jig so that the blade cuts just inside the pencil line.

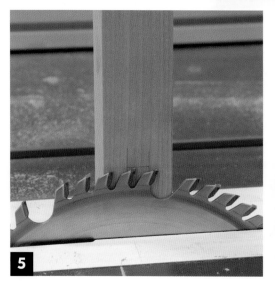

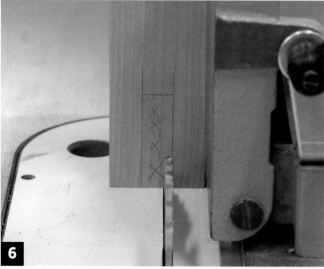

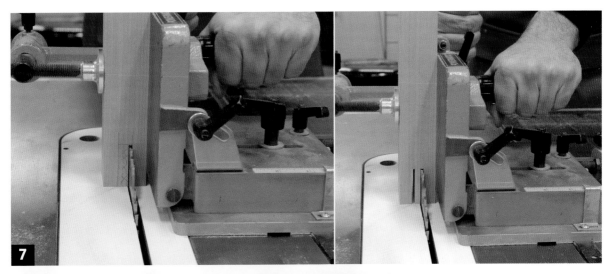

7. Make the cut, then rotate the workpiece around and cut the other side. Using the tenoning jig this way means the open mortise will be perfectly centered.

8. If multiple workpieces need this same joint, cut them all before adjusting the tenoning jig to remove the remainder of the stock.

9. Making multiple passes with a single blade may result in a shoulder that needs a bit of cleanup. Use a chisel to smooth the shoulder as needed. Be sure to chisel from both sides of the joint so the shoulder is square and clean on both sides.

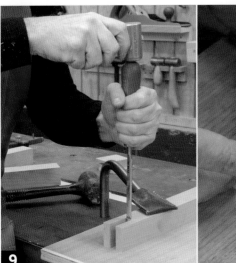

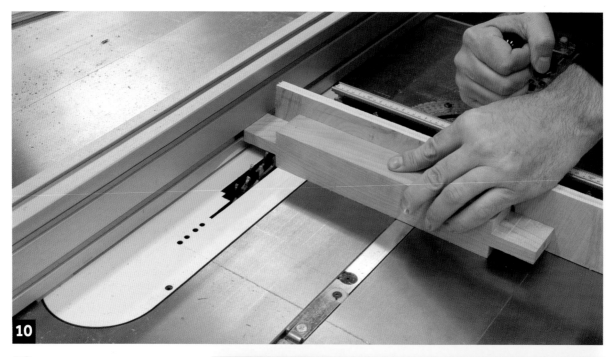

10. **The male portion of the** joint can be cut using any of the methods described for cutting a tenon in Chapter 3. Shown is using the dado stack and a miter gauge to sneak up on the fit, using the female portion of the joint for testing.

11. **The joint should be snug** but shouldn't require a hammer to assemble.

12. **With glue on all adjoining** surfaces, the joint is first clamped in two directions to fully seat the shoulders. An additional clamp is added to the face of the joint to help squeeze the parts together.

13. **Once the glue is dry, the** surfaces can be planed smooth and perfectly flush.

THE FEMALE PORTION OF THE JOINT

There are numerous methods you can use to produce the female portion of a bridle joint depending on your available tools and personal preferences. Here are a few examples.

Tablesaw with Tall Fence + Support Board

Much like the half-lap version of this operation, this isn't my favorite method, but it can work in a pinch. Make a cut with each face against the fence to center the mortise area. The fence is then moved to clear out the material between the initial cuts.

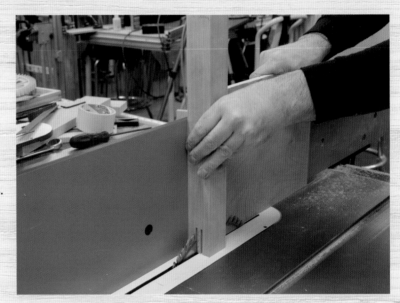

Tablesaw with Dado Stack + Tenoning Jig

This method is very similar to the one outlined above, only the dado blade is capable of removing the material in one or two passes. Depending on the side of the bridle joint, it could be a lot to ask of the dado blade to remove it all in one shot. If that's the case, make two to three cuts, raising the blade each time.

Bandsaw

With a sharp blade and a well-tuned bandsaw, the cheek cuts can be made in short order. Take care not to go past the shoulder scribe line.

Clear out the material between the initial cut lines free-hand.

The shoulder can then be cleaned up at the workbench with a chisel.

If necessary and if room allows, the cheeks can be cleaned up with a chisel.

T-SHAPED BRIDLE JOINT

The *T*-shaped bridle joint is very similar to a mortise and tenon, except two sides of the mortise are open. It makes a beautiful exposed joint on the edges or door or frames of any kind.

TOOLS

Adjustable square
Marking knife
Tablesaw with dado blade
Clamps

1. After laying out the location where the workpieces will intersect and making sure it's square, clamp the two workpieces together and mark the joint location. Using a marking knife, scribe along the sides of the female workpiece.

TIP Not all marking knives are created equal. For joinery, I like a marking knife that has one flat face and one beveled face. I put the flat face against the reference surface for the most accurate scribe lines possible.

2. Cut the female portion of the joint using your preferred method as described on pages 174 and 175.

3. With the miter gauge in place, adjust the fence and the miter gauge stop so the blade is lined up with the insides of the two layout lines.

4. With the dado blade installed, raise the blade height so it's just below the layout line on the male workpiece.

5. Cut the joint on one face, progressing from one stop to the other.

6. Test the fit using the female workpiece. Adjust the stops if needed until the female piece fits well between the shoulders of the male workpiece.

7. Now that you're confident in the location of the shoulder to shoulder distance, cut the other side of the workpiece.

8. Apply glue to adjoining surfaces and assemble the joint.

9. Apply clamping pressure across the joint as well as sandwiching the joint together.

10. Once the glue is dry, plane the surface smooth and flush.

ALTERNATIVE METHODS

MALE PORTION OF THE JOINT

Tablesaw with Miter Gauge + Single Blade

If you don't have a dado blade, a single blade can certainly be used to make the male portion of the *T*-shaped bridle joint. Just nibble away the stock one kerf-width per pass. Do a little handplane cleanup on the surface to smooth out the grooves left behind by the tablesaw blade.

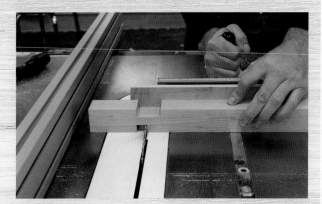

Router Table with Miter Gauge + Straight Bit

The router table is a great alternative to the tablesaw when cutting the male portion of the *T*-shaped bridle joint. With a sacrificial auxiliary fence on the miter gauge, the resulting cuts should be smooth and tearout-free.

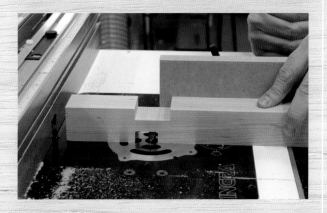

Chapter 5

DOVETAILS

Dovetails are often regarded as the pinnacle of woodworking joinery due to the incredible strength and the obvious beauty of the joint. Dovetails also appear rather complex to the uninitiated; executing the joint successfully is something of a rite of passage. If you can cut dovetails, you probably have more than just a passing casual interest in the craft. Although we tend to show off our dovetails like a new mother with her bundle of joy, the ironic fact is that dovetails were originally hidden because their true value lies in their mechanical strength. You might find them in drawers hidden behind a false front or in casework covered by moldings or a top. Most times, the dovetails even had large gaps that would make a 21st century YouTuber screech in horror. Whether hidden and gappy or in your face and "toight" like a tiger, the dovetail remains an excellent joinery option for drawers, boxes, and casework.

THROUGH DOVETAILS

Through dovetails are often used in drawers and casework. The pins and tails nest together with the end grain of both boards visible in the final assembled joint. I usually cut the tails first, followed by the pins. The "hand-cut look" can also be achieved using the bandsaw and some clever tips and tricks.

TOOLS

Cutting gauge
Adjustable square
Bevel gauge
Dovetail saw
Fret or coping saw
Chisel
Mallet
Marking knife

1. Label the parts appropriately, being sure the terms you use are as easy to understand as possible—front, back, sides, inside, outside, etc. If you're making a drawer, the sides are tail boards and the fronts and backs are the pin boards.

2. Set a cutting gauge to the thickness of the boards to be joined.

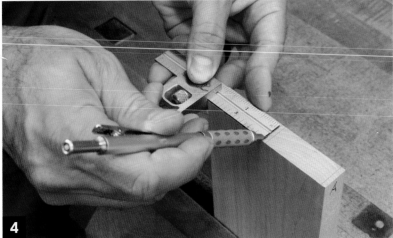

3. Scribe the shoulder line on all four sides of each board. Set the marking gauge aside to retain this setting. You'll need it later.

4. Lay out the tails in a way that pleases the eye. Keep in mind, whatever you do here will likely repeat on other corners of the drawer, case, box, or whatever you're making. In this example, an adjustable square establishes a simple, symmetrical layout: one small pin socket in the middle and two half-pin sockets on the outside, resulting in two large tails.

5. Using a bevel gauge set to the desired angle, begin extending the pencil lines down the face of the board. The angle can be anything from 6 to 12°. Go with the angle that looks best given the material and the application.

6. **Clearly mark the waste** between the tails (pin sockets) as this helps avoid cutting on the wrong side of the line.

7. **With the saw blade in the** waste area right next to the pencil line, begin cutting at the appropriate angle and stop before hitting the shoulder scribe line.

8. **Make the remaining cuts in** the same fashion. You can use your thumb as a stop to start the cut.

9. **If you don't follow your lines** perfectly, don't worry. No one will notice if your tail angles aren't perfectly consistent. You do, however, need to make sure your saw is perpendicular to the face of the board for each cut.

10. Using a coping or fret saw, carefully cut away the waste between the tails while staying just above the shoulder line.

11. With the board on its side, cut away the outer half-pin socket waste.

12. Using a chisel, establish the final shoulder by placing a chisel in the shoulder scribe line and chopping down into the base of the tail. Cut into the corner horizontally along the tail wall to finish off the shoulder. Repeat this process on the other half-pin socket.

13. **Check the sides of the tails** to make sure they're square to the face. If not, use a chisel to make slight corrections.

14. **Clamp the tail board to the** workbench with a piece of scrap underneath and use a small chisel to clean up the shoulder. Place the chisel in the scribe line and chop about halfway through the thickness of the board. Don't chop all the way through because you might over-cut the scribe line.

15. **Not all chisels are created** equal. A specialized dovetail chisel (below left, with a traditional chisel on right) can be useful for getting into tight pin sockets because the sides are sharply beveled and won't cut into the tails.

16. **Check all shoulder areas for** square and adjust as needed.

17. **Prepare the pin board for** layout by applying a layer of blue tape to the end grain and trimming the perimeter excess. I first saw these blue tape techniques demonstrated by Glen Huey and Mike Pekovich.

18. **On the tail board, place two** strips of tape on the inside face, just covering the shoulder scribe line. Use the cutting gauge to slice through the tape. The double layer of tape can now act as a fence that's perfectly in line with the dovetail's shoulder.

19. **Clamp the pin board** vertically (outside facing out) so it sits just a bit above the surface of the workbench.

20. **Lay the tail board (outside** facing up) on top of the scrap and push the tail board forward until the blue tape fence makes contact. Use a straight edge to help keep the boards aligned.

21. **Use hand pressure to hold** the tail board down and use a sharp thin marking knife to scribe along each tail. Make several light passes to ensure you cut completely through the tape.

22. Remove the tape between the pins. The remaining tape serves as a guide for cutting the pins.

23. Extend the guide lines down to the shoulder scribe line with a fine pencil. These will serve as a visual aid that will help you saw straight, or at least know when you're not sawing straight.

24. Place the saw against the blue tape in the waste area. The tape is not only a visual marker, it can actually help align the saw perfectly for the start of the cut.

25. Use a fret saw or coping saw to remove the waste between the pins.

26. **Clamp the pin board to the** workbench with a piece of scrap underneath and use a chisel to clean up the shoulders. Place a chisel in the scribe line and chop about halfway through the thickness of the board.

27. **Flip the board and repeat** the cleanup process from the other side.

28. **Use a square to confirm** the shoulders are flat or slightly concave. If the shoulder is convex and has a bump, that extra material will interfere with the fit. Pare it away with a chisel.

29. Inspect the pin walls to see if there is any material sitting proud of the blue tape. If so, pare it away.

30. Test fit. The joy of the blue tape layout trick is that the dovetails often fit perfectly the first time. If the fit is too snug, find the offending material and pare it away.

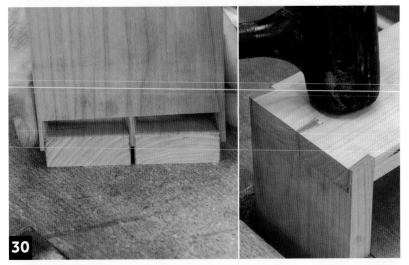

31. Remove the blue tape, add some glue, assemble the joint, and clean up with some sanding after the glue dries.

32. One of my dovetails seems to have a small chunk missing from one of the pins. To fix it, glue in a small sliver of scrap, roughly chiseled to the shape of the missing piece and hammer it in with some glue.

> **TIP** Small pins, as pictured here, are beautiful and show the world that they were cut by hand. But for structural weight-bearing applications, the tiny pins might present a weak point. I reserve small pin configurations for decorative boxes and drawers.

33. **Once dry, the patch is** trimmed and sanded; the flaw is nearly undetectable.

34. **With a little finish, the joint** comes to life!

A CLOSER LOOK

HANDCUT VS MACHINE CUT

Because dovetails are so popular, there are numerous jigs and fixtures on the market devoted solely to producing the perfect dovetail. I personally own a Leigh D4R and it's easily one of the best jigs on the market. I find these jigs helpful when I have a lot of dovetails to cut or when the dovetails are being used purely for their structural integrity. But in my opinion, machine-cut dovetails have one major weakness: they are limited by the size of the typical router bit. So if you're looking to create smaller more refined pins—a hallmark of the handcut dovetail—it's just not possible with a router. The only way to achieve tiny pins is to cut by hand or use some variation of handcut as I'll demonstrate. This also begs the question, "Why do we want smaller pins?" That answer is simple: Because they look awesome!

   Another reason I feel handcut dovetails are worth your time to master is because the skills you'll acquire are transferable to other areas of woodworking. Knowing how to mark a line, cut to it, then finesse that line with chisels is a set of skills that will benefit your woodworking in general. So, consider the practice an investment in your woodworking career.

BANDSAW ALTERNATIVE

A bandsaw is great to cut tails. With a sharp high-tooth-count blade and the help of a simple angle fixture, the bandsaw saves time and gives very consistent results. And because the bandsaw blade is thin, you can still achieve small pins and a handcut look.

TOOLS

Angle fixture
Angle gauge
Bandsaw

1. Make a simple angle fixture from any sheet good material you have laying around. One side should be square and the other side should be cut at your desired dovetail angle. This example uses 7°. Drill a few holes for a dowel pin that will serve as a stop.

2. Adjust the bandsaw fence so the blade is positioned just inside the tail pencil line. This puts the blade completely in the waste of the cut.

3. With the workpiece against the dowel stop, carefully make the cut. The workpiece and the jig should move together, so hold them securely with your hands.

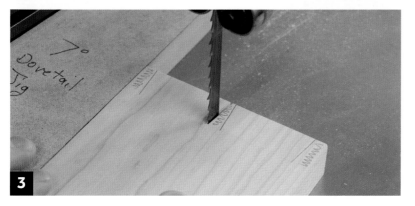

4. Flip the workpiece and make a second cut. This should result in a perfectly centered pin socket.

5. Adjust the fence for the next cut, once again placing the blade just inside the tail line in the waste.

6. Flip the workpiece and cut again, resulting in two symmetrical half-pin sockets.

7. Carefully remove the waste material with several light cuts on the bandsaw.

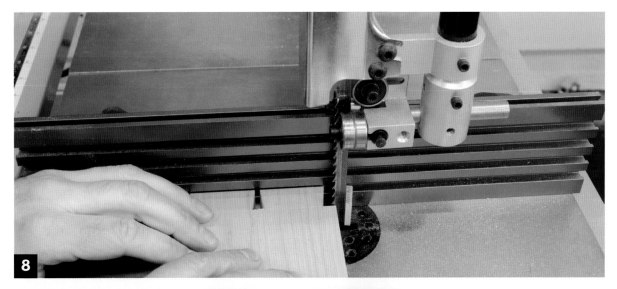

8. The half-pin sockets can be cleared out by using the fence as a stop. While it's possible to align the blade right on the scribe line, it's usually safer to leave a bit of material so you don't risk over-cutting. Clean up the shoulders using a chisel at the workbench.

9. The tail sockets between the pins can be cut at the bandsaw instead of using a coping saw or fret saw. Just take care not to accidentally cut into the pins.

A CLOSER LOOK

KNOW THE LIMITS

You might be wondering if you can also cut the pins at the bandsaw. You can, but it's not quick and simple like the tail operation. In order to cut the pins, the bandsaw table needs to tilt to the appropriate angle, in both directions. Most bandsaw tables only tilt in one direction. To overcome this, you would need to build a sled that holds the workpiece at the correct angle for each cut.

FIX THOSE GAPS

Gaps happen. No matter how skilled you are, at some point you'll accidentally cut a pin or tail too small or you'll trim off too much material while hunting for that piston-fit. Unfortunately, even a small gap can be a monumental eyesore to the perfectionist. Resist the urge to repair using wood filler or sawdust and glue. Both of these options will fill the gap, the but the repair is nearly always visible and obvious after finishing. Glue doesn't accept finish and fillers just don't look like wood. Here's how you can fix gaps in your dovetails.

1. **Evaluate the flaw and try** to find a piece of scrap with similar color and grain.

2. **Draw the angle through the** piece of scrap as a cut guide.

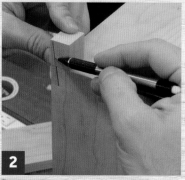

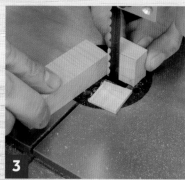

3. **Carefully cut the scrap** piece along the drawn angle. Watch your fingers!

4. **As an alternative, if you** don't want to fuss about grain direction, you can simply saw off a fine sliver of material at the tablesaw.

5. **Take the cut piece to a** piece of sandpaper to smooth and flatten it out.

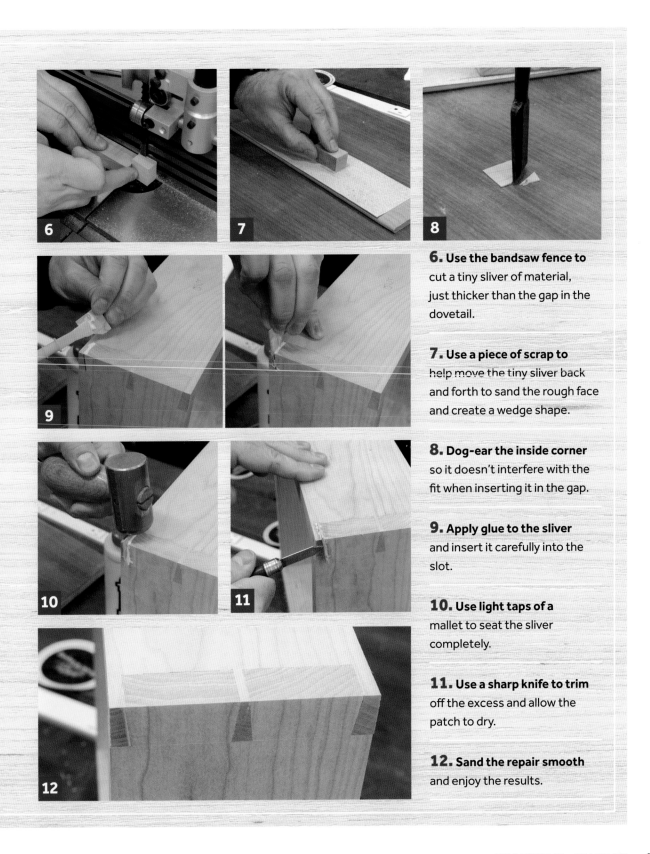

6. **Use the bandsaw fence to** cut a tiny sliver of material, just thicker than the gap in the dovetail.

7. **Use a piece of scrap to** help move the tiny sliver back and forth to sand the rough face and create a wedge shape.

8. **Dog-ear the inside corner** so it doesn't interfere with the fit when inserting it in the gap.

9. **Apply glue to the sliver** and insert it carefully into the slot.

10. **Use light taps of a** mallet to seat the sliver completely.

11. **Use a sharp knife to trim** off the excess and allow the patch to dry.

12. **Sand the repair smooth** and enjoy the results.

HALF-BLIND DOVETAILS

A common variation of the dovetail joint is the half-blind dovetail. The most common application for this joint is in a drawer where the maker doesn't want the dovetails to be visible from the front. Cutting the tails is pretty much the same process as through dovetails, but the pin board has some significant differences.

TOOLS

Cutting gauge
Bevel gauge
Dovetail saw
Chisel
Mallet
Adjustable square
Clamps
Marking knife
Straightedge
Router
Straight router bit

1. Set a cutting gauge to the thickness of the tail board.

2. Scribe the shoulder line on the inside face of the pin board.

3. Decide how much pin board material you want in front of your tails (setback) and use the gauge to scribe across the pin board end grain, referencing from the inside face. There should be at least a ⅛" setback, but depending on the size of the parts, you might go larger.

4. Use the same setting on the cutting gauge to scribe all four sides of the tail board.

5. Lay out the tails in a way that is pleasing to the eye. To keep the tails symmetrical, use an adjustable square to mark in from each edge. For this example, there will be two large tails, with a small pin socket at the center and two small half-pin sockets on the ends. If this is your first time, you will want to make your pin sockets larger so they aren't quite as fragile.

6. Using a bevel gauge set to the desired angle, begin extending the pencil lines down the face of the board. The angle can be anything from 6 to 12 °. Go with the angle that looks best given the material and the application.

7. Clearly mark the waste between the tails (pin sockets); this helps avoid cutting on the wrong side of the line.

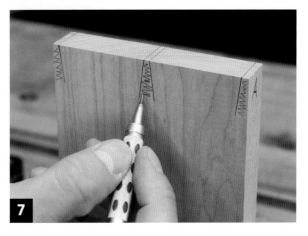

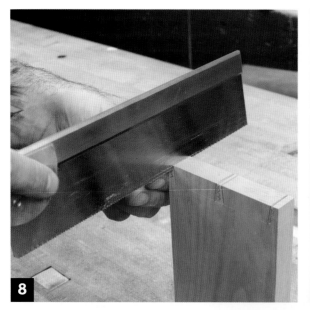

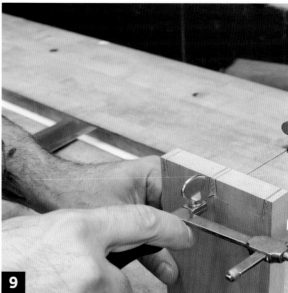

8. **With the saw blade in the** waste area right next to the pencil line, begin cutting at the appropriate angle and stop before hitting the shoulder scribe line.

9. **Using a coping saw or fret** saw, carefully cut away the waste between the tails while staying just above the shoulder line.

10. **With the board on its side,** cut away the outer half-pin socket waste.

11. **Using a chisel, establish the** final shoulder surface by placing a chisel in the shoulder scribe line and chopping down.

12. **Check the sides of the tails** to make sure they're square to the face. If not, use a chisel to make slight corrections.

13. **Clamp the tail board to the** workbench with a piece of scrap underneath and use a small chisel to clean up the shoulder. Place the chisel in the scribe line and chop about halfway through the thickness of the board. Don't chop all the way through or you might over-cut the scribe line.

14. **On the tail board, place** two strips of blue tape on the inside of the board so they cover the shoulder scribe line, then use the cutting gauge to slice through the tape. The tape will now serve as a fence.

15. **Clamp the pin board** vertically (outside facing out) so it's flush with a piece of scrap stock. The scrap raises the work slightly, making it easier to transfer the marks.

16. **Lay the tail board (outside** facing up) on top of the scrap and push the tail board forward until the blue tape fence makes contact. Use a straight edge to help keep the boards aligned.

17. **Use hand pressure to hold** the tail board down and use a sharp thin marking knife to scribe along each tail. Be sure to scribe along the end grain of the tails too. Make several light passes to ensure you cut completely through the tape.

18. **Remove the tape between** the pins. The remaining tape serves as a guide for cutting the pins.

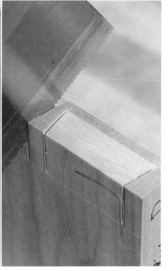

19. **Place the saw against the** blue tape in the waste of the cut, tilting the heel of the saw down slightly. This cut has to be made at a 45° angle to prevent cutting into the pin walls and shoulders.

20. **You can remove the waste** with a chisel if you want, but it is generally much easier and faster to use a router and a straight bit. Set the bit depth to the scribe line and carefully hog out the material between the pins, keeping a safe distance from the saw cut lines. You can use the other workpiece to help balance the router.

21. **Use a chisel to remove the** remaining stock in front of the pin walls, working back to the tape lines.

22. Establish the shoulders by placing the chisel in the scribe line and chopping down.

23. Test fit the joint and make any adjustments needed to the pin walls.

24. Assemble the joint with glue and remove the blue tape.

25. Apply some finish to see the joint in all its glory.

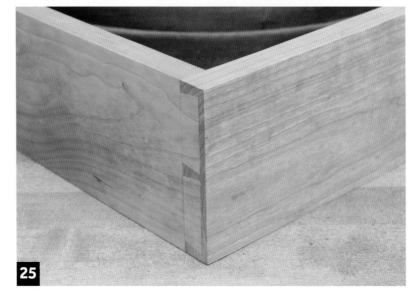

TAPERED SLIDING DOVETAILS

While technically a dovetail, the sliding dovetail actually has more in common with a dado than with a traditional dovetail. Because wood quickly swells with exposure to water-based glue, most sliding dovetails work better if they're tapered. If you can cut a tapered sliding dovetail, the nontapered version is a piece of cake, so we'll focus on the tapered version here.

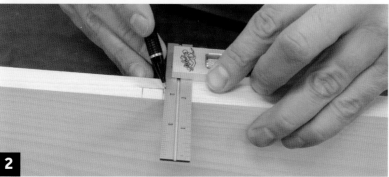

TOOLS

Adjustable square
Router
Dovetail router bit
Push pad

1. Arrange the adjoining pieces and label them clearly.

2. Lay out the dovetail slot location on the edge of the board. No need to draw in the dovetail angles since those will be dictated by the bit we use.

3. Set up the router table with your dovetail bit. Shown here is a ½" diameter with a 14° angle. Adjust the fence and bit height so the dovetail bit sits inside the layout lines.

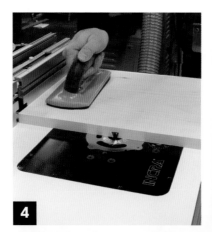

4. **Cut the straight dovetail slot.**

5. **Keeping the stock flush** against the fence ensures a dovetail slot that is straight and true—a must if the joint is to go together smoothly.

6. **Introduce a taper to the slot** by taping a small 1/16" thick shim to the back end of the board.

7. **By skewing the board slightly** and re-cutting the dovetail, the front of the dovetail remains the same and gradually tapers out on one side as it approaches the back of the board.

8. Cut the mating dovetail on the adjoining piece using the same bit at the same height setting. The fence should be moved so that only part of the bit cuts into the board and a shim of the same thickness as the previous shim is added to the back side of the board. Be sure to close up your fence so that the gap is no wider than the width of the shim, otherwise the shim could fall into the gap and mess up the dovetail.

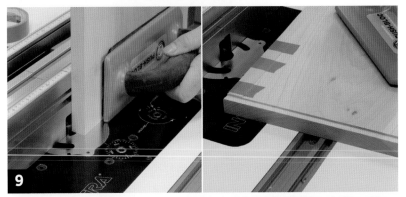

9. Sneak up on the fit by taking a light pass on each face, testing the fit, moving the fence, and cutting again. Repeat as needed until the dovetails slide.

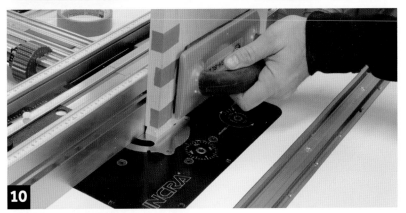

10. The fit should be too tight, so adjust the fence slightly and take two more passes. Remember, any adjustment you make to the fence results in removing twice that amount of material.

11. Test the fit and cut again if necessary.

12. The fit should start loose and then tighten up when it's fully seated.

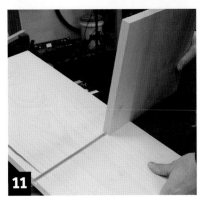

METRIC CONVERSIONS

In this book, lengths are given in inches. If you want to convert those to metric measurements, please use the following formulas:

Fractions to Decimals

$\frac{1}{8}$ = .125

$\frac{1}{4}$ = .25

$\frac{1}{2}$ = .5

$\frac{5}{8}$ = .625

$\frac{3}{4}$ = .75

Imperial to Metric Conversion

Multiply inches by 25.4 to get millimeters

Multiply inches by 2.54 to get centimeters

Multiply yards by .9144 to get meters

For example, if you wanted to convert $1\frac{1}{8}$ inches to millimeters:

1.125 in. x 25.4mm = 28.575mm

And to convert $2\frac{1}{2}$ yards to meters:

2.5 yd. x .9144m = 2.286m

CONVERSIONS

Fractions to Decimal Equivalents (Inches)

1/64	.015625	33/64	.515625
1/32	.031250	17/32	.531250
3/64	.046875	35/64	.546875
1/16	.062500	9/16	.562500
5/64	.078125	37/64	.578125
3/32	.093750	19/32	.593750
7/64	.109375	39/64	.609375
1/8	.125000	5/8	.625000
9/64	.140625	41/64	.640625
5/32	.156250	21/32	.656250
11/64	.171875	43/64	.671875
3/16	.187500	11/16	.687500
13/64	.203125	45/64	.703125
7/32	.218750	23/32	.718750
15/64	.234375	47/64	.734375
1/4	.250000	3/4	.750000
17/64	.265625	49/64	.765625
9/32	.281250	25/32	.781250
19/64	.296875	51/64	.796875
5/16	.312500	13/16	.812500
21/64	.328125	53/64	.828125
11/32	.343750	27/32	.843750
23/64	.359375	55/64	.859375
3/8	.375000	7/8	.875000
25/64	.390625	57/64	.890625
13/32	.406250	29/32	.906250
27/64	.421875	59/64	.921875
7/16	.437500	15/16	.937500
29/64	.453125	61/64	.953125
15/32	.468750	31/32	.968750
31/64	.484375	63/64	.984375
1/2	.500000	1	1.00000

Inches to Millimeters (Fractions to Decimal Equivalents)

1/64	0.396875	33/64	13.09688
1/32	0.793750	17/32	13.49375
3/64	1.190625	35/64	13.89063
1/16	1.587500	9/16	14.28750
5/64	1.984375	37/64	14.68438
3/32	2.381250	19/32	15.08125
7/64	2.778125	39/64	15.47813
1/8	3.175000	5/8	15.87500
9/64	3.571875	41/64	16.27188
5/32	3.968750	21/32	16.66875
11/64	4.365625	43/64	17.06563
3/16	4.762500	11/16	17.46250
13/64	5.159375	45/64	17.85938
7/32	5.556250	23/32	18.25625
15/64	5.953125	47/64	18.65313
1/4	6.350000	3/4	19.05000
17/64	6.746875	49/64	19.44688
9/32	7.143750	25/32	19.84375
19/64	7.540625	51/64	20.24063
5/16	7.937500	13/16	20.63750
21/64	8.334375	53/64	21.03438
11/32	8.731250	27/32	21.43125
23/64	9.128125	55/64	21.82813
3/8	9.525000	7/8	22.22500
25/64	9.921875	57/64	22.62188
13/32	10.31875	29/32	23.01875
27/64	10.71563	59/64	23.41563
7/16	11.11250	15/16	23.81250
29/64	11.50938	61/64	24.20938
15/32	11.90625	31/32	24.60625
31/64	12.30313	63/64	25.00313
1/2	12.70000	1	25.40000

ABOUT THE AUTHOR

Marc Spagnuolo has been an online woodworking content producer known as The Wood Whisperer since 2006. He is a podcaster, video producer, and woodworking enthusiast.

Author of the book *Hybrid Woodworking,* he has also contributed articles and video content to FineWoodworking.com, *Popular Woodworking Magazine, Woodcraft Magazine,* and *WOOD Magazine.*

Marc is the founder and owner of The Wood Whisperer Guild, an online woodworking school featuring video instruction from top woodworkers. He has taught classes at the Marc Adams and William Ng woodworking schools, and has given presentations at Fine Woodworking Live, AWFS, IWF, and local clubs throughout the country.

Marc is a comics and video game nerd, and enjoys life in Denver with his wife, Nicole, and their two children, Mateo and Ava. Follow Marc on on his Web site thewoodwhisperer.com. Purchase detailed woodworking courses at woodwhispererguild.com. Follow him on social media *@woodwhisperer.*

ACKNOWLEDGMENTS

While writing this book, I would occasionally confront a technical snag; I relied on a few key people to help me resolve those issues. Thanks for the assist: Shannon Rogers, Matt Cremona, and Matthew Teague.

Thanks to our friend John Funk—webmaster, graphic designer, and business consultant—who single-handedly made the technical aspects of our book pre-order campaign possible.

Thank you to my beautiful and brilliant wife, Nicole, for keeping our children (Mateo and Ava) occupied while I toiled away cutting joints and taking photos in the shop.

Thanks to the woodworking community for supporting my work, making me laugh, and challenging me to constantly improve.

Finally, I need to thank my mom Lorna (a.k.a. TWWMom). She taught me how to write, how to argue a point effectively, and how to clip coupons (though I choose not to).

INDEX

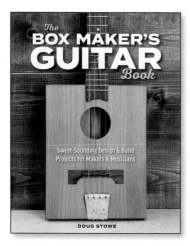
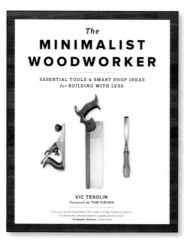
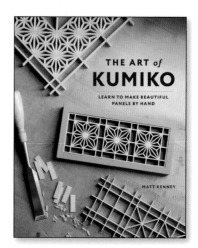
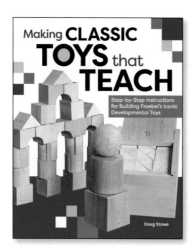
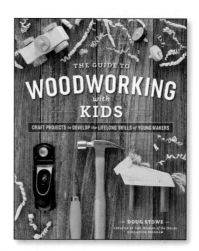